First World War
and Army of Occupation
War Diary
France, Belgium and Germany

19 DIVISION
58 Infantry Brigade
Duke of Edinburgh's (Wiltshire Regiment)
6th Battalion
5 January 1915 - 31 May 1918

WO95/2093/2

The Naval & Military Press Ltd
www.nmarchive.com
Published in association with The National Archives

Published by

The Naval & Military Press Ltd

Unit 10 Ridgewood Industrial Park,

Uckfield, East Sussex,

TN22 5QE England

Tel: +44 (0) 1825 749494

www.naval-military-press.com

www.nmarchive.com

This diary has been reprinted in facsimile from the original. Any imperfections are inevitably reproduced and the quality may fall short of modern type and cartographic standards.

© Crown Copyright
Images reproduced by permission of The National Archives, London, England, 2015.

Contents

Document type	Place/Title	Date From	Date To
Heading	WO95/2093-2		
Heading	19th Division 56th Infy Bde 6th. Bn Wiltshire Regt Jly 1915-May 1918 To 14 Div 42 Bde		
Heading	56th Inf. Bde. 19th Div. Battn. Disembarked Boulogne From England 20.7.15 War Diary Battn. The Wiltshire Regiment. July (20.7.15-30.7.15) 1915 Mar 18		
War Diary	Boulogne	20/07/1915	21/07/1915
War Diary	Nordausques	21/07/1915	22/07/1915
War Diary	Arques	23/07/1915	23/07/1915
War Diary	Lambres	24/07/1915	30/07/1915
Heading	56th Inf. Bde. 19th Div. War Diary 6th Battn. The Wiltshire Regiment. August (31.7.15-31.8.15) 1915		
War Diary	Haverskerque	31/07/1915	04/08/1915
War Diary	Cornet Malo	05/08/1915	16/08/1915
War Diary	Laventie	17/08/1915	18/08/1915
War Diary	Laventie	19/08/1915	26/08/1915
War Diary	Cornet Malo	27/08/1915	29/08/1915
War Diary	Paradis	30/08/1915	31/08/1915
Heading	58th Inf. Bde. 19th Div. War Diary War Diary 6th Battn. The Wiltshire Regiment September 1915		
War Diary		01/09/1915	30/09/1915
Heading	58th Inf. Bde. 19th Div. War Diary 6th Battn. The Wiltshire Regiment October 1915		
War Diary	Cuinchy (In The Trenches)	01/10/1915	07/10/1915
War Diary	Le Quesnoy	08/10/1915	08/10/1915
War Diary	L'Epinette	09/10/1915	24/10/1915
War Diary	Le Touret	25/10/1915	31/10/1915
Heading	58th Inf. Bde. 19th Div. War Diary 6th Battn. The Wiltshire Regiment November 1915		
War Diary	In The Trenches	01/11/1915	02/11/1915
War Diary	Richbourg St Vaast	03/11/1915	07/11/1915
War Diary	Le Touret.	08/11/1915	17/11/1915
War Diary	La Tombe Willot.	18/11/1915	25/11/1915
War Diary	Le Sart	26/11/1915	30/11/1915
Heading	56th Inf. Bde. 19th Div. War Diary 6th Battn. The Wiltshire Regiment. December 1915		
War Diary	Le Sart.	01/12/1915	03/12/1915
War Diary	Vielle Chapelle	04/12/1915	04/12/1915
War Diary	Rue Des Chavatte	05/12/1915	10/12/1915
War Diary	Le Touret	11/12/1915	18/12/1915
War Diary	Penin Marriage	19/12/1915	22/12/1915
War Diary	In The Trenches	23/12/1915	26/12/1915
War Diary	Croix Barbee	27/12/1915	31/12/1915
Heading	6th Welsh Vol : 7 Jan 16		
Heading	War Diary Of 6th (S) Btn Wiltshire Regt. From 1st January To 31st January 1916 Volume No 7		
War Diary	In The Trenches	01/01/1916	04/01/1916
War Diary	Le Touret	05/01/1915	18/01/1915
War Diary	In The Trenches	18/01/1916	22/01/1916
War Diary	Le Touret	23/01/1916	28/01/1916

War Diary	Le Sart	24/01/1916	31/01/1916
Heading	War Diary Of 6 Bn Wiltshire Regiment. From 1st February 1916 To 29th February 1916 Volume No. 8		
War Diary	Le Sart.	01/02/1916	15/02/1916
War Diary	Pont Du Hem.	16/02/1916	17/02/1916
War Diary	In The Trenches	18/02/1916	19/02/1916
War Diary	Pont Du Hem	20/02/1916	21/02/1916
War Diary	In The Trenches	22/02/1916	23/02/1916
War Diary	La Gorgue	24/02/1916	29/02/1916
Heading	War Diary Of 6th (Service) Btn Wiltshire Regiment. From 1st March 1916 To 31st March 1916 Volume 9.		
War Diary	In The Trenches	01/03/1916	04/03/1916
War Diary	Rue Des Chavatte	05/03/1916	07/03/1916
War Diary	Paradis	08/03/1916	14/03/1916
War Diary	Croix Barbee	15/03/1916	17/03/1916
War Diary	In The Trenches	18/03/1916	21/03/1916
War Diary	Croix Barbee	22/03/1916	23/03/1916
War Diary	Merville	23/03/1916	25/03/1916
War Diary	Kings Road Ruedes Chavatte.	26/03/1916	27/03/1916
War Diary	In The Trenches	28/03/1916	31/03/1916
Heading	War Diary Of 6th (Service) Bn Wiltshire Regiment From 1st April 1916 To 30th April 1916 Volume 10.		
War Diary	Rue Des Chavattes	01/04/1916	04/04/1916
War Diary	In The Trenches	05/04/1916	08/04/1916
War Diary	Kings Road Rue Des Chavattes	09/04/1916	11/04/1916
War Diary	Rue Des Chavattes	12/04/1916	12/04/1916
War Diary	In The Trenches	13/04/1916	14/04/1916
War Diary	Rue Des Chavatte.	17/04/1916	17/04/1916
War Diary	Kings RD Rue Des Chavattes	18/04/1916	19/04/1916
War Diary	Les Loibes	20/04/1916	20/04/1916
War Diary	Robecq	21/04/1916	22/04/1916
War Diary	Quernes	23/04/1916	30/04/1916
Heading	War Diary Of 6th (S) Bn Wiltshire Regiment. From 1st May To 31st May 1916 Volume II		
Miscellaneous	From Officer Commanding 6th Bn Wiltshire Regt To D.A.G. 3rd Echelon	01/06/1916	01/06/1916
War Diary	Quernes	01/05/1916	08/05/1916
War Diary	Flesselles	09/05/1916	29/05/1916
War Diary	Gorenflos.	30/05/1916	30/05/1916
War Diary	Millancourt	31/05/1916	31/05/1916
Heading	War Diary Of 6th Bn Wiltshire Regiment From 1st June 1916 To 30th June 1916. Vol 12		
War Diary	Millancourt	01/06/1916	10/06/1916
War Diary	Gorenflos St. Vast	11/06/1916	14/06/1916
War Diary	Rainneville	15/06/1916	15/06/1916
War Diary	Albert	16/06/1916	30/06/1916
Heading	58th Inf. Bde 19th Div War Diary 6th Battn. The Wiltshire Regiment. July 1916		
Heading	War Diary Of 6th Bn Wiltshire Regt From 1st July 1916 To 31st July 1916 Volume 13 Vol 13		
War Diary	Albert	01/07/1916	08/07/1916
War Diary	Baizieux	09/07/1916	20/07/1916
War Diary	Becourt Wood	21/07/1916	21/07/1916
War Diary	Mametz	22/07/1916	23/07/1916
War Diary	In The Trenches	24/07/1916	30/07/1916
War Diary	La Houssoye	31/07/1916	31/07/1916

Heading	58th Brigade 19th Division 1/6th Battalion Wiltshire Regiment August 1916			
War Diary	La Houssoye		01/08/1916	03/08/1916
War Diary	Cocquerel		04/08/1916	06/08/1916
War Diary	Nr Kemmel		07/08/1916	07/08/1916
War Diary	In The Trenches		08/08/1916	13/08/1916
War Diary	Nr Kemmel		14/08/1916	31/08/1916
Heading	War Diary Of 6th (S) Bn Wiltshire Regt. From 1st To 30th Sept. 1916 Volume 15			
War Diary	Kemmel		01/09/1916	04/09/1916
War Diary	De Seule		05/09/1916	08/09/1916
War Diary	Chapelle Rompue		09/09/1916	23/09/1916
War Diary	Merris		24/09/1916	30/09/1916
Heading	War Diary Of 6th Bn, Wiltshire Regt. From 1st Oct To 31st Oct 1916 Volume-16			
War Diary	Merris		01/10/1916	13/10/1916
War Diary	In The Trenches		14/10/1916	16/10/1916
War Diary	Vauchelles		17/10/1916	17/10/1916
War Diary	Herrisart		18/10/1916	22/10/1916
War Diary	Bouzincourt		23/10/1916	23/10/1916
War Diary	Crucifix Corner		23/10/1916	26/10/1916
War Diary	In The Trenches		26/10/1916	31/10/1916
Heading	War Diary Of 6th (S) Bn Wiltshire Regt From 1/11/16 To 30/11/16 Volume 17			
War Diary	N Aveluy		01/11/1916	02/11/1916
War Diary	In The Trenches		03/11/1916	05/11/1916
War Diary	Aveluy		06/11/1916	11/11/1916
War Diary	In The Trenches		12/11/1916	14/11/1916
War Diary	Nr Authille Wood		14/11/1916	15/11/1916
War Diary	In The Trenches		15/11/1916	17/11/1916
War Diary	N Aveluy		17/11/1916	20/11/1916
War Diary	In The Trenches		21/11/1916	22/11/1916
War Diary	N Aveluy		23/11/1916	23/11/1916
War Diary	Warloy		24/11/1916	24/11/1916
War Diary	Doullens		25/11/1916	25/11/1916
War Diary	Boisbergues		26/11/1916	30/11/1916
Heading	War Diary Of 6th (S) Bn Wiltshire Regiment. From 1st To 31st December 1916 Volume 18.			
War Diary	Boisbergues		01/12/1916	31/12/1916
Heading	War Diary Of 6th (S) Bn The Wiltshire Regiment From 1st To 31st January 1917 Volume 19			
War Diary	Boisbergues		01/01/1916	09/01/1916
War Diary	Beauval		10/01/1917	11/01/1917
War Diary	Hebuterne		12/01/1916	15/01/1916
War Diary	Sailly		16/01/1917	23/01/1917
War Diary	Hebuterne		24/01/1917	27/01/1917
War Diary	Sailly		28/01/1917	31/01/1917
Heading	War Diary Of 6th (S) Bn Wiltshire Regiment. From 1st To 28th February 1917 Volume 20			
War Diary	In The Trenches		01/02/1917	01/02/1917
War Diary	Hebuterne		01/02/1917	04/02/1917
War Diary	Sailly		05/02/1917	20/02/1917
War Diary	Louvencourt		21/02/1917	28/02/1917
Heading	War Diary Of 6th (S) Bn. Wiltshire Regt From 1st To 31st March 1917 Volume 21			
War Diary	Louvencourt		01/03/1917	01/03/1917

War Diary	Euston Camp	02/03/1917	02/03/1917
War Diary	Puisieux	03/03/1917	03/03/1917
War Diary	Euston Camp	04/03/1917	04/03/1917
War Diary	Yew Camp Bus	05/03/1917	10/03/1917
War Diary	Beauval	11/03/1916	11/03/1916
War Diary	Neuvillette	12/03/1917	13/03/1917
War Diary	Nuncq	14/03/1917	14/03/1917
War Diary	Bours	15/03/1917	16/03/1917
War Diary	Auchy-Au-Bois	17/03/1917	18/03/1917
War Diary	Boisenghem	19/03/1917	19/03/1917
War Diary	Strazeele	20/03/1917	20/03/1917
War Diary	Rouge Croix	21/03/1917	22/03/1917
War Diary	Race Croix	23/03/1917	31/03/1917
Heading	War Diary Of 6 (s) Bn Wiltshire Regiment. From 1st April To 30th April 1917 Volume 22		
War Diary	Ridge Wood	01/04/1917	04/04/1917
War Diary	In The Trenches (Diependaal Sector).	04/04/1917	04/04/1917
War Diary	In The Trenches	05/04/1917	08/04/1917
War Diary	De Zon Camp	09/04/1917	16/04/1917
War Diary	In The Trenches	17/04/1917	18/04/1917
War Diary	Carnarvon Camp	19/04/1917	19/04/1917
War Diary	Mont Des Cats	20/04/1917	29/04/1917
War Diary	Scottish Camp	30/04/1917	30/04/1917
Heading	6th Bn Wiltshire Regt. War Diary Volume 23 May 1917 Vol 23		
War Diary	Ypres	01/05/1917	04/05/1917
War Diary	Zillebeke	04/05/1917	13/05/1917
War Diary	Vancouver Camp	13/05/1917	13/05/1917
War Diary	Mont.Des Cats	14/05/1917	15/05/1917
War Diary	Wallon. Cappell	16/05/1917	16/05/1917
War Diary	Longvenesse	17/05/1917	17/05/1917
War Diary	Nordausques	18/05/1917	25/05/1917
War Diary	Curragh Camp	26/05/1917	26/05/1917
War Diary	Weston Camp	27/05/1917	31/05/1917
Heading	War Diary Of 6th (S) Bn Wiltshire Regiment From 1st To 30th June 1917 Volume 24		
War Diary	Weston Camp	01/06/1917	01/06/1917
War Diary	In The Trenches	02/06/1917	03/06/1917
War Diary	Murrumbidgee Camp	04/06/1917	05/06/1917
War Diary	Weston Camp	06/06/1917	06/06/1917
War Diary	In The Line	07/06/1917	09/06/1917
War Diary	Bois Carre	10/06/1917	10/06/1917
War Diary	Oostverne Wood	11/06/1917	18/06/1917
War Diary	Curragh Camp	19/06/1917	19/06/1917
War Diary	Nr Bailleul	20/06/1917	30/06/1917
Heading	War Diary Of 6th (s) Bn Wiltshire Regiment. From 1st To 31st July 1917 Volume 25		
War Diary	Nr Bailleul	01/07/1918	02/07/1918
War Diary	Nr Kemmel	03/07/1918	10/07/1918
War Diary	Dammstrasse	11/07/1918	11/07/1918
War Diary	In The Trenches	12/07/1918	15/07/1918
War Diary	Denys Wood	15/07/1918	18/07/1918
War Diary	N Locre	19/07/1918	30/07/1918
War Diary	N Estaminet Corner	31/07/1918	31/07/1918
Heading	War Diary Of 6th (s) Bn Wiltshire Regiment. From 30th July 1917 To 31st August 1917 Volume 26		

War Diary	In The Trenches	30/07/1917	07/08/1917
War Diary	N Bailleul	08/08/1917	11/08/1917
War Diary	Seninghem	12/08/1917	31/08/1917
Heading	War Diary Of 6 (s) Bn Wiltshire Regt. From 1st To 30 Sept 1917 Volume 27		
War Diary	N Berthen	01/09/1918	10/09/1918
War Diary	Nr Kemmel	11/09/1917	11/09/1917
War Diary	Spoil Bank	12/09/1917	14/09/1917
War Diary	N Kemmel	15/09/1917	18/09/1917
War Diary	In The Trenches	19/09/1917	19/09/1917
War Diary	Opaque Wood	20/09/1917	23/09/1917
War Diary	Bois Confluent.	24/09/1917	25/09/1917
War Diary	Bois Carree	26/09/1917	30/09/1917
Heading	War Diary Of 6' (S) Bn. Wiltshire Regt. From 1st To 31st October 1917 Volume 28		
War Diary	Spoil Bank	01/10/1917	03/10/1917
War Diary	In The Trenches	04/10/1917	07/10/1917
War Diary	Spoil Bank.	08/10/1917	11/10/1917
War Diary	Rossignol Camp	12/10/1917	19/10/1917
War Diary	Spoil Bank	20/10/1917	24/10/1917
War Diary	In The Trenches	24/10/1917	28/10/1917
War Diary	Nr Brasserie	28/10/1917	31/10/1917
Heading	War Diary Of 6 (S) Bn. Wiltshire Regiment From 1st To 30 Nov 1917 Volume 29		
War Diary	Nr Brasserie	01/11/1917	06/11/1917
War Diary	Rossignol Camp	07/11/1917	09/11/1917
War Diary	Stazeele	10/11/1917	11/11/1917
War Diary	Lynde	12/11/1917	30/11/1917
Heading	War Diary Of 6th (S) Bn Wiltshire Regiment From 1st To 31st December 1917 Volume 30		
War Diary	Tilques	01/12/1917	02/12/1917
War Diary	Lynde	03/12/1917	07/12/1917
War Diary	Blairville	08/12/1917	08/12/1917
War Diary	Gommecourt	09/12/1917	09/12/1917
War Diary	Etricourt	10/12/1917	11/12/1917
War Diary	Nr Ribecourt	12/12/1917	22/12/1917
War Diary	Havricourt Wood	23/12/1917	24/12/1917
War Diary	Nr. Ribecourt	25/12/1917	31/12/1917
Heading	War Diary Of 6 (S) Bn Wiltshire Regt From 1st To 31 Jany 1918 Volume 31		
War Diary		01/01/1918	03/01/1918
War Diary	Ribecourt	04/01/1918	05/01/1918
War Diary	Hindenburg Line	06/01/1918	09/01/1918
War Diary	In The Trenches	09/01/1918	14/01/1918
War Diary	In The Line	15/01/1918	15/01/1918
War Diary	Valley Trench	16/01/1918	16/01/1918
War Diary	Hawes Camp	17/01/1918	22/01/1918
War Diary	In The Trench	22/01/1918	24/01/1918
War Diary	Hawes Camp	25/01/1918	31/01/1918
Heading	War Diary Of 6 (s) Bn Wiltshire Regt. Volume 32 From 1st To 28 Feb 1918 Vol 32		
War Diary	In The Line	01/02/1918	01/02/1918
War Diary	Vallulart Camp	02/02/1918	05/02/1918
War Diary	In The Line	06/02/1918	13/02/1918
War Diary	Nr Rocquigny	14/02/1918	23/02/1918
War Diary	Nr Haplincourt	24/02/1918	28/02/1918

Heading	19th Division. 58th Infantry Brigade. War Diary 6th Battalion Wiltshire Regiment March 1918		
Heading	War Diary Of 6 (S) Bn Wiltshire Regiment. From 1st To 31st March 1918 Volume 33		
War Diary	Sanders Camp	01/03/1918	01/03/1918
War Diary	Haplincourt	03/03/1918	19/03/1918
War Diary	Sanders Camp	20/03/1918	31/03/1918
Miscellaneous			
Miscellaneous	Narrative Of Operations C Wiltshire Regt.	27/03/1918	27/03/1918
Miscellaneous	Ask Division Of The require way thing further with require to lessons		
Miscellaneous	Lessons Learnt	02/04/1918	02/04/1918
Miscellaneous	Operations 21/28 March 1918	21/03/1918	21/03/1918
Heading	58th Brigade. 19th Division. War Diary Not Received By Historical Section Narrative Of Events 1/6th Battalion Wiltshire Regiment April 1918		
Miscellaneous	H.Q. 58th Inf. Bde.	00/04/1918	00/04/1918
Miscellaneous	6th Wiltshire Yeomanry Battn. The Wiltshire Regt.	25/04/1918	25/04/1918
Miscellaneous	HQ. 58th Inf Bde.	25/04/1918	25/04/1918
Miscellaneous	6th Wiltshire Yeomanry Battn The Wiltshire Regt	25/04/1918	25/04/1918
Miscellaneous	Approximate Casualties Of The 6th Wilts R Between The 10th April To 20th April 1918 Appendix	10/04/1918	10/04/1918
Heading	30th Division 21st Infy Bde 6th Bn Wilts Regt May 1918		
Heading	War Diary Of 6th (Service) Battn. Wiltshire Regiment May 1918 Volume 35		
Miscellaneous	6th Battalion. Wiltshire Regt.		
War Diary	Herzeele	13/05/1918	13/05/1918
War Diary	Hazebrouck 6th 1/100,000	13/05/1918	13/05/1918
War Diary	Lederzeele	14/05/1918	14/05/1918
War Diary	Hazebrouck 5A	15/05/1918	15/05/1918
War Diary	Mellen Ville Dieppe 1/100,000	16/05/1918	24/05/1918
War Diary	Mellen Ville Maps Dieppe 1/100,000	25/05/1918	31/05/1918
Heading	6th Wiltshire		

WO 95/2093(2)

19TH DIVISION
58TH INFY BDE

6TH. BN WILTSHIRE REGT
JLY 1915 - MAY 1918

TO 17 DIV 42 BDE

58th Inf.Bde.
19th Div.

Battn. disembarked
Boulogne from
England 20.7.15.

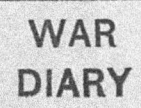

6th BATTN. THE WILTSHIRE REGIMENT.

J U L Y

(20.7.15 - 30.7.15)

1 9 1 5

Army Form C. 2118

6th Wilts.

WAR DIARY

~~INTELLIGENCE SUMMARY~~

(Erase heading not required.)

Instructions regarding War Diaries and Intelligence Summaries are contained in F. S. Regs., Part II. and the Staff Manual respectively. Title Pages will be prepared in manuscript.

Place	Date	Hour	Summary of Events and Information	Remarks and references to Appendices
BOULOGNE	July 20	3 a.m.	Battalion arrived at OSTROHOVE CAMP from ENGLAND	
NORDAUSQUE	" 21	6.30 AM	Battalion left by entrainment at PONT DES BRIQUES	
"	"	1.0 PM	Arrived and went into billets, having marched from point of detrainment at AUDRUICQ	
"	" 22	—	Halt & Training	
ARQUES	" 23	5.0 PM	Billeted, having marched from NORDAUSQUE	
LAMBRES	" 24	2.30 PM	Marched from ARQUES & went into billets. Inspected by the C.in.C. on the march	
"	" 25	—	Halt. Church Parade	
"	" 26	—	Halt - Training	
"	" 27	—	Halt - Training	
"	" 28	—	Halt - Training	
"	" 29	—	Halt - Training. Visited by Sir Douglas Haig	
"	" 30	—	Halt - Training	

58th Inf.Bde.
19th Div.

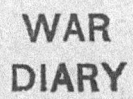

6th BATTN. THE WILTSHIRE REGIMENT.

A U G U S T

(31.7.15 - 31.8.15)
1 9 1 5

1/4 Wiltshire Regt.

WAR DIARY or INTELLIGENCE SUMMARY

(Erase heading not required.)

Army Form C. 2118

Instructions regarding War Diaries and Intelligence Summaries are contained in F. S. Regs., Part II. and the Staff Manual respectively. Title Pages will be prepared in manuscript.

Place	Date 1915	Hour	Summary of Events and Information	Remarks and references to Appendices
HAVERSKERQUE	July 31	3 PM	Arrived and went into billets, having marched from LAMBRES 3/09 Pte Joacp WS died.	Ry 239.
"	Aug. 1	—	Halt - Church Parade.	R239.
"	Aug. 2	—	Halt - Training	R239.
"	Aug. 3	—	Halt - Training	
"	Aug. 4	—	Halt - Training. Inspected by Lt Gen Sir James Willcocks (G.O.C. Indian Corps).	R239.
CORNET MALO	Aug. 5	10.45 am	Arrived & went into billets, having marched from HAVERSKERQUE.	L239.
"	Aug. 6	—	Halt - Training	L239.
"	Aug. 7	—	Halt - Training	L239.
"	Aug. 8	—	Halt - Church Parade cancelled owing to wet weather.	L239.
"	Aug. 9	—	Halt - Training	L239.
"	Aug. 10	—	Halt - Training	L239.
"	Aug. 11	—	Halt - Training	L239.
"	Aug. 12	—	Halt - Training. Brigade night concentration practised	L239.
"	Aug. 13	—	Halt - Training	L239.
"	Aug. 14	—	Halt - Training	
"	Aug. 15	—	Halt - Church Parade.	L239.
"	Aug. 16	—	Halt - Training	L239.
LAVENTIE	Aug. 17	12 pm	Arrived and went into billets, having marched from CORNET MALO. Capt Gingell with 2 Platoons (85 men) went into trenches for instruction occupied by 2nd LEICESTERSHIRES (GARHWAL BRIGADE) at FAUQUISSART (M.24.b)(48 hours)	Reference:— MAP SHEET 36
"	Aug. 18	—	2 Working Parties "C" Coy worked on LE DRUMEZ POST. At night 2 Platoons "A" Coy, "B" Coy, "D" Coy Machine Gun Section. Revet Machine Gun Section Emplacement, worked on Communication Trench on M.18.a.b. & between WANGERIE and RUE MASSELOT)	Reference:— MAP SHEET 36

SHEET 1 August 1915.

6th Wiltshire Regt

WAR DIARY
or
INTELLIGENCE SUMMARY
(Erase heading not required.)

Army Form C. 2118

Instructions regarding War Diaries and Intelligence
Summaries are contained in F.S. Regs., Part II.
and the Staff Manual respectively. Title Pages
will be prepared in manuscript.

Place	Date 1915	Hour	Summary of Events and Information	Remarks and references to Appendices
LAVENTIE	Aug.19	—	"C" Coy worked on LE DRUMEZ POST: N° 3 and 4 Platoons "A" Coy relieved N°s 1 and 2. The Machine Gun Section went into the trenches for instruction	MAP SHEET. 36 LRg.
"	Aug.20	—	"C" Coy worked on LE DRUMEZ POST. "B" and "D" Coy at WANGERIE POST. 2 Platoons "A" Coy at ROAD BEND POST. 1 man "A" Coy wounded	LRg.
"	Aug.21	—	"B" and "C" Coys at WANGERIE POST: "A" and "D" Coy on Tramway at L'EPINETTE FARM: The man wounded on 20th died. 4 men wounded	MAP SHEET 36 AF.B.3.15.d/27/15 LRg.
"	Aug.22	—	2 Platoons of "B" Coy went into the trenches for instruction with the 1st/3rd LONDONS. 2 Platoons of "C" Coy with the LEICESTERS: "D" Coy continued work on the Tramway. "A" Coy continued work on LE DRUMEZ POST.	MAP SHEET 36 AF.B. 2.15.d/27/15 LRg.
"	Aug.23	—	"A" Coy worked on WANGERIE POST. Composite Coy worked on LE DRUMEZ POST. The Battalion had working parties on LE DUMEZ, RUE TILLEROY, and the Tramway: Right half Coy of "B" and "C" Coy were relieved by their left half Coys. 1 man killed, 1 wounded	MAP SHEET 36 AF.B. 2.15.d/27/15 LRg
"	Aug.24	—	Work was continued on Tramway: three days & the four days previous the Battalion also made barb wire trail obstacles (about 600 pu down) 1 man killed. D Coy went into trenches, 2 Platoons to the LEICESTERS, and 2 Platoons to the LONDONS	MAP SHEET 36 AF.B.2.15.d/27/15 LRg
"	Aug.25	—	"B" and "C" Coys evacuated the trenches. "A" Coy continued work on Tramway & trench at RUE TILLEROY. A working party was employed on LE DRUMEZ POST. 1 man mortally wounded, 2 wounded	MAP SHEET 36 AF.B.2.15.d/27/15

SHEET. 2.   AUGUST. 1915.

6th Wiltshire Regt

WAR DIARY
or
INTELLIGENCE SUMMARY
(Erase heading not required.)

Army Form C. 2118

Instructions regarding War Diaries and Intelligence
Summaries are contained in F. S. Regs., Part II.
and the Staff Manual respectively. Title Pages
will be prepared in manuscript.

Place	Date 1915	Hour	Summary of Events and Information	Remarks and references to Appendices
LAVENTIE	Aug 26	—	The Battalion moved from LAVENTIE to billets at CORNET MALO. "D" Coy. was relieved from the Trenches during the evening & marched independently. Whilst on the Battalion was marching a few shells burst in LAVENTIE. The Battalion however sustained no casualties. Total casualties during stay in LAVENTIE :— 4 killed, 7 wounded.	MAP SHEET 36 & 36A AF B215-9P7½ MAP SHEET 36A
CORNET MALO	Aug 27 Aug 28	—	Half-Training Half-Training	MAP SHEET 36A
"	" 29	—	The Battalion marched into fresh billets at PARADIS and EGLISE where it remained for the night.	1156A
PARADIS	" 30	—	The Battalion with remainder of 58th Brigade marched into GORRE WOOD from whence, in the evening, it took over a line of trenches in the QUINQUE RUE Nr FESTUBERT from the 9th Devons, part of the 7th Division. 3 Companies in firing line support and one in Reserve. A quiet night was spent	1197 MAP SHEET 36NW BETHUNE COMBINED
	" 31	—	No change in position. enemy snipers were on at different times at day and night, "A" Company being specially busy in improving new saps and trenches at ROTHSAY BAY. The enemy were very quiet	

SHEET 3. AUGUST 1915.

58th Inf.Bde.
19th Div.

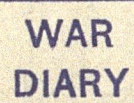

6th BATTN. THE WILTSHIRE REGIMENT.

S E P T E M B E R

1 9 1 5

WAR DIARY
or
INTELLIGENCE SUMMARY
(Erase heading not required.)

Army Form C. 2118

6th (S) Battn Wiltshire Regt

Instructions regarding War Diaries and Intelligence Summaries are contained in F.S. Regs., Part II. and the Staff Manual respectively. Title Pages will be prepared in manuscript.

Place	Date 1915	Hour	Summary of Events and Information	Remarks and references to Appendices
	1 Sept		The day passed very quietly. The enemy fired a few rifle grenades, one of which failed to explode. Were sent to the Brigade for examination. Working parties continued to improve trenches during the day - one man was wounded during the evening.	MAP SHEET BETHUNE COMBINED
	2 "		Day very quiet. Working parties as usual. One man wounded.	Do.
	3 "		Very wet, which hindered the working party. Work carried on at ROTHSAY BAY and two new communication trenches. Enemy very quiet.	Do.
	4 "		Wet. Working parties as usual. Enemy quiet except for rifle grenades being fired in early morning and evening. Two men slightly wounded.	Do.
	5 "		Weather fine. Enemy quiet except for occasional shots with rifle grenades. Work commenced on new support trench between Richmond & Abbey Roads. One man wounded on listening post.	Do.
	6 "		Enemy sent several rounds of shrapnel rifle grenades over trenches in the morning. 3 men wounded. Remainder of day very quiet	Do

Sheet No 1. September 1915.

WAR DIARY or INTELLIGENCE SUMMARY

Army Form C. 2118

(Erase heading not required.)

Instructions regarding War Diaries and Intelligence Summaries are contained in F. S. Regs., Part II. and the Staff Manual respectively. Title Pages will be prepared in manuscript.

Place	Date 1915	Hour	Summary of Events and Information	Remarks and references to Appendices
	7 to 8 Sept.		Enemy quiet both these days. Our artillery more active - mostly "ranging". Working parties continued working on above mentioned trenches. 3 men wounded by shrapnel fire.	MHP 317987 BETHUNE eembaineo.
	9-10		Enemy more active sending trenchmortars rifle grenades over in greater quantity. 5 men wounded. Work continued in improving parapet, making new communication & support trench. Work on support trench was delayed as enemy had apparently found its range & frequently shelled it. A draft of 50 men arrived from 6th Battn. on evening of 10th.	
	11		Enemy quiet except for trenchmortars fired about 8% on the morning. Work continued on the trenches between to back of Sandbags. The work was greatly hindered. Capt. Smith & Lieut. Freeman sent in a useful report on the trenches.	
	12		Work continued on the two new communication trenches.	
	13		Enemy very quiet. Weather continues fine. Very little firing on either side. During the night however the enemy were very active and a great deal of machine gun & rifle fire was done. There were no casualties however.	

WAR DIARY
or
INTELLIGENCE SUMMARY
(Erase heading not required.)

Army Form C. 2118

Place	Date	Hour	Summary of Events and Information	Remarks and references to Appendices
	14 Sept		Things normal – work continued on improving trenches and sandbags, wire and finishing off new communication trenches. No casualties. Enemy very quiet indeed.	MAP SHEET BETHUNE COMBINED.
	15 "			
	16 "		Battalion moved on Wednesday evening in billets on reserve "G" Coy occupying posts at Rue de Cailloux, Lockhert, Le Plantin various small ammunition stores. Rest of Battalion were in dug outs on the intermediate lines near Stamnet Corner. Battalion employed on improving Schuhir Trench.	
	17 "			
	18 "			
	19 "			
	20 "		On Thursday night 2 Officers were hit whilst superintending work. Lieut. Moulton being killed & Lt. Jackivaite being wounded. There were no casualties amongst the men. Weather very fine. They'S generally quiet. On Sunday morning the enemy fired shells at Kennedy Fork Road.	
	21 "		Battalion occupied the northern extremity of the intermediate lines which were greatly improved, many dug outs being built on the ground. On Thursday evening various posts including 50 men of "C" Company were relieved by the South Wales Borderers. The enemy caused no trouble whatever. A few shells were sent over the Northern end of our line but never fell near.	
	22 "			
	23 "			

WAR DIARY
or
INTELLIGENCE SUMMARY
(Erase heading not required.)

Army Form C. 2118

Place	Date	Hour	Summary of Events and Information	Remarks and references to Appendices
	Sept 24		The Battalion moved from entrenched lines to reserve trenches in evening in anticipation of active operations. A very wet night was spent owing to lack of accomodation on dug outs.	
	25		At 5.15 am on 25th an order was received that the attack would commence at 5.50 with asphyxiating gas and smoke candles. The assault signal was given at 6/30 by rockets from Brigade Office. The 58th Brigade's objective was the German lines just in front and rear of Rue d'Ouvert. The Welch on our right supported by the Cheshires. The Welsh Fusiliers to our front supported by ourselves made the assault which was carried out by advancing through the gas. Owing to the gas not taking effect, the division on our right were unable to take the "Crater" ridge with the result that the enemy on our front were able to bring enfilade fire on our troops (the safe were poor) and the attack was repulsed. A & B did not come into action but D Company on the left went over the parapet and attacked. They were soon held up and suffered heavy casualties. Capt. Wykes & Lt. Wise were wounded, 2nd Lt. Moore & Coleman were killed and other ranks were 17 killed, 17 missing and 46 wounded. 2nd Lt. Truman took over charge of the Company and after holding on for a considerable	

1875. Wt. W593/826. 1,000,000 4/15 J.B.C. & A. A.D.S.S./Forms/C. 2118.

WAR DIARY or INTELLIGENCE SUMMARY

(Erase heading not required.)

Army Form C. 2118

Place	Date Sept	Hour	Summary of Events and Information	Remarks and references to Appendices
	25		(continued) time withdrew the remainder of the Company with considerable judgment to our original firing line under orders from Major Stanley. The enemy remained quiet. The Battalion took over the firing line from the Fusiliers who had suffered heavy loses. Owing to the wet weather considerable difficulty was experienced in bringing back the wounded and clearing up the trenches.	
	26 & 27		Both these days were occupied in bringing in the wounded of both Battalions. On the evening of the 26 the Fusiliers left the front line and the Battalion took over the trenches with Lifle Regt on its right and Bamton Road on its left. B & C Companies in the firing line, "A" Company Colonys Redoubt, Neuport Line and "D" Company in reserve. The Casualties of the action were 3 Officers killed, 2 wounded and other ranks 22 killed, 70 wounded and 20 missing. Lieut Cook was killed while endeavouring to use his machine gun. He had been previously wounded but had gallantly advanced again and was killed while firing his gun.	

WAR DIARY or INTELLIGENCE SUMMARY

Army Form C. 2118

Place	Date	Hour	Summary of Events and Information	Remarks and references to Appendices
	Sept. 28 & 29		Weather rainy both these days. Both days spent in salvage repairing trenches.	
	30.		On evening of 29th the Battalion was relieved by North Staffordshire Regiment of 57 Brigade. Owing to wet weather the relief was a very long & tedious one. The Battalion was marched into LOCON by Companies arriving between 4 & 5 a.m. The morning of the 30th was spent in readjusting billets – one Company managed to get baths & clean clothing. At 11 am orders were received that the Brigade was to hold itself in readiness to move. At 2 p/c the Battalion marched from LOCON & picked up remainder of Brigade at LE HAMEL & continued its march to ANNEQUIN & CAMBRIN. The Brigade then took over trenches from 6th Brigade, the Brigade then Battalion holding a line from the CANAL on the left & RIDLEY STREET on right exclusive. "D" Company took up the left, "C" the centre and "A" the right, "B" Company remaining in support. The enemy were very quiet. The Casualties on the 25th were 4 Officers killed & one wounded, other ranks 24 killed, 16 missing & 73 wounded.	

58th Inf.Bde.
19th Div.

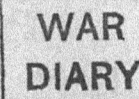

6th BATTN. THE WILTSHIRE REGIMENT.

O C T O B E R

1 9 1 5

WAR DIARY or INTELLIGENCE SUMMARY

(Erase heading not required.)

Army Form C. 2118

Place	Date Oct.	Hour	Summary of Events and Information	Remarks and references to Appendices
CUINCHY (IN THE TRENCHES)	1st 15.	—	Owing to relief taking place in dark & in very bad weather, the day was spent in reorganising the platoons & cleaning up. Col. Jeffreys was badly burnt by accident & had to go to 16 Field Ambulance. Major Hanbury took over Command.	MAP SHEET 36 A. LR1.
"	2nd		Weather very fine. Work was continued on firing line parapets. At 8 pm the enemy exploded a mine near Cockshy Lane. The enemy did not follow it up and working parties soon got to work and communication was soon restored between our right & centre Companies.	LR1
"	3rd		Weather fine. "B" Company relieved "A".	F99
"	4,5 & 6/5		These 3 days were spent with assistance from 9 Cheshires & 9 Welch by night in improving the new Crater trench & parapets in general which are still in a bad state of repair. The casualties of the Battalion to this date are :- 5 Officers killed, 3 wounded. Other ranks 38 killed & 16 missing & 101 wounded.	LR1

October 10/15. Sheet No. 1

Army Form C. 2118

WAR DIARY
or
INTELLIGENCE SUMMARY
(Erase heading not required.)

Instructions regarding War Diaries and Intelligence Summaries are contained in F. S. Regs., Part II. and the Staff Manual respectively. Title Pages will be prepared in manuscript.

Place	Date 1915	Hour	Summary of Events and Information	Remarks and references to Appendices
CUINCHY	Oct 7		Battalion was relieved by 2nd Queens who took over our line from Kialy walk to Bexley Rd. We took over from Coldstream Guards from over line Coldly Lane to the Church. The relief was done in daylight. The Battn. went into billets as L'Epinette for the night.	BETHUNE COMBINED SHEET F39
LE QUESNOY	" 8		The Battn. left Le Quesnoy and marched into billets at L'Epinette.	F39
L'EPINETTE	" 9		Battalion went into Bath rooms for baths.	F39
	" 10		Church parade. "D" Coy went to Bath rooms. Remainder of Battalion resting.	
	" 11 to 17		Three days were spent in route marching, re-equipping the Battalion, bomb throwing practice with light bombs & machine gun classes. On Tuesday the Battn. was taken to La Gorgue for baths. One Officer & 2 men went on leave on Saturday.	LBG
	" 18		Battn. marched into Billets at Neuve Chapelle	F39 F39
	" 19		Half Raining	F39
	" 20		Battn. moved into rest billets at LA TOMBE WILMOT.	F39
	" 21 " 22 " 23		Three days were spent in Route Marching, bomb throwing & machine gun classes. On the 22nd the Battn. went to Locon for Baths. "D"	F39 F39
	" 24		Battalion moved to fresh billets in Reserve at LE TOURET. "D" Company did not take over their billets until the evening when they marched to Rue de L'Epinette relieved a company of the 2nd D. W. R.	F39

October 1915. Sheet No. 2.

WAR DIARY or INTELLIGENCE SUMMARY

Army Form C. 2118

(Erase heading not required.)

Instructions regarding War Diaries and Intelligence Summaries are contained in F. S. Regs., Part II. and the Staff Manual respectively. Title Pages will be prepared in manuscript.

Place	Date Oct	Hour	Summary of Events and Information	Remarks and references to Appendices
LE TOURET	25/26		Three days working parties commenced improving ARC LINE & RICHMOND TRENCH. On the 26th two men of "B" Coy were wounded by shell fire. Bomb throwing classes – weather very wet.	BETHUNE BOMBING SCHOOL SHEET END
"	27.		Work continued on PIPE LINE & RICHMOND TRENCH. Bomb throwing classes. One N.C.O. & 3 men on Lewis Machine Gun Course. 4 "C" Coy went to Rouen for baths.	£B9
"	28/29/30		These days were spent on Billets at Le Touret. Working parties were supplied every night in the firing line. No casualties.	£B9 £B9
"	31 "		Battalion took over section IND. B.2 from the 9" Welch – A Coy on the left, "C" Coy in the centre, "D" Coy and one platoon of "B" on the right. Remainder of "B" Coy Sapper & Headquarters reserve.	£B9

H. B. Hartley
Major commdg 6th Wilts ×

October 1915 – P. T. O. No. 3.

58th Inf.Bde.
19th Div.

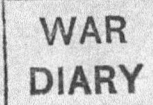

6th BATTN. THE WILTSHIRE REGIMENT.

N O V E M B E R

1 9 1 5

WAR DIARY or INTELLIGENCE SUMMARY

Army Form C. 2118

(Erase heading not required.)

Instructions regarding War Diaries and Intelligence Summaries are contained in F. S. Regs., Part II. and the Staff Manual respectively. Title Pages will be prepared in manuscript.

Place	Date 1915	Hour	Summary of Events and Information	Remarks and references to Appendices
IN THE TRENCHES. RICHBOURG ST VAAST.	Nov 1			BETHUNE COMBINED SHEET
	" 2		Weather was extremely bad these two days the trenches became in a very bad state and a great majority of the dug outs fell in.	
	" 4		Large working parties were sent up and an attempt was made to repair and in many places reconstruct the fire trenches and communication trenches. The Batts. suffered one killed and five wounded and a great many men sick with trench foot. The enemy	PB9.
	" 5			
	" 6		were very quiet except for occasional sniping. The new was received that 2nd Lieut Sherman had been awarded the military Cross	PB9
	" 7		Battalion relieved by 9th Welch Regt. and went into billets at LE TOURET. A draft of 21 men, mostly sick and wounded and who had recovered, were sent to join the Battalion.	
LE TOURET.	" 8			PB9
	" 9		These days were spent in billets at LE TOURET. Working parties were required both day and night. about 300 daily. The weather was wet + a good deal of discomfort was experienced.	
	" 10			PB9
	" 11		The Battalion relieved 9th Welch on 11ND 26.	PB9
	" 12			
	" 13		Very wet cold day which prevented much improvement to the trenches. Weather greatly improved and hard hard frosts were experienced at night. Working parties of 100 men each every morning from the 5th Brigade who were in Reserve at LOCON were found to be of great assistance in consequence of which and the absence of shelf fire. Owing to the state of the communication trenches and the Battalion Being under strength very little work could be done in	PB9
	" 14			
	" 15			PB9
	" 16			

October 1915. Sheet No 1

Army Form C. 2118

WAR DIARY
or
INTELLIGENCE SUMMARY
(Erase heading not required.)

Instructions regarding War Diaries and Intelligence Summaries are contained in F. S. Regs., Part II. and the Staff Manual respectively. Title Pages will be prepared in manuscript.

Place	Date Nov	Hour	Summary of Events and Information	Remarks and references to Appendices
	17th		In the daytime no large parties of troops could be sent moved with safety up to the firing line as the communication trenches were impassable. All ration brought however here to the bacon up almost. Battalion relieved by 8th Gloucester Regiment and marched into Billets at LA TOMBE WILLOT since the 12th were 2 killed & 3 wounded. There was a great deal of trench foot and many men went sick with it.	BETHUNE contained sheet
LA TOMBE WILLOT	18th		Day spent in cleaning up and making up deficiencies of clothing equipment etc. 2 Companies had baths at LOCON	F84
	19th 20		Battalion continued to get re-equipped and special attention was paid to smartening up the men from the effects of the trenches. A good deal of bathing was done.	F84
	21st		Church Parade and baths.	F84
	22nd		Working party of 60 men was sent to the trenches - remainder of Battalion had Company drill and short route marches.	F86
	23rd		Battalion moved at 4.30pm to billets at LE SART near MERVILLE	F84
	24th		2nd Lieutenants Leyland, Mortimer, Kemp arrived. Major Stevens	F84
	25th		2nd Lieut. Packard took C.Sn of the Brigade joined. The Battalion and proceeded on leave to England for 10 days.	F84

WAR DIARY
or
INTELLIGENCE SUMMARY

(Erase heading not required.)

Army Form C. 2118

Place	Date Nov	Hour	Summary of Events and Information	Remarks and references to Appendices
LE SART	26		Platoon training and route marching.	£89
	27		Platoon training Do.	£89
	28		Church Parade	£89
	29		Company Training	£89
	30			

Walter King Lt Col.
6th Bt. Wiltshire Regt.

58th Inf.Bde.
19th Div.

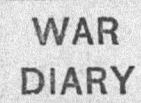

6th BATTN. THE WILTSHIRE REGIMENT.

DECEMBER

1915

WAR DIARY or INTELLIGENCE SUMMARY

(Erase heading not required.)

Army Form C. 2118

Place	Date Dec.	Hour	Summary of Events and Information	Remarks and references to Appendices
LE SART	1st		Company training - bombing demonstration in the afternoon.	BETHUNE/M COMBINED SHEET. 36A
	2nd		Company training for "D" Company - remaining companies at PONT DUHEM drawing.	36A
	3rd		Headquarters, "D" Company & transport moved to VIEILLE CHAPELLE. A-B&C Companies arrived at VIEILLE CHAPELLE in the evening from PONT DU HEM.	36A
VIEILLE CHAPELLE RUE DES CHAVATTE	4th		Battalion moved from billets at VIEILLE CHAPELLE to RUE DES CHAVATTE	36A
	5th		Sunday - rest.	36A
	6th		Cleaning billets, refitting and company drill.	36A
	7th		Battalion relieved 9th R.W.F. in trenches 1800yds over the line from QUINQUE RUE to FARM POST - D & B Companies in the firing line - C & A in reserve. Headquarters on RUE DES BOIS.	36A
	8th 9th 10th		Battalion holds the trenches. Our artillery carried out bombardment & to which the enemy replied very little. Casualties were 1 man killed and 2 wounded. Companies relieved every 24 hours.	36A
LE TOURET	11th		Battalion relieved by 8th Gloucesters and went to billets at EMPERORS ROAD.	36A

December 1915 Sheet 1

WAR DIARY or INTELLIGENCE SUMMARY

Army Form C. 2118

Instructions regarding War Diaries and Intelligence Summaries are contained in F. S. Regs., Part II. and the Staff Manual respectively. Title Pages will be prepared in manuscript.

(Erase heading not required.)

Place	Date Dec.	Hour	Summary of Events and Information	Remarks and references to Appendices
LE TOURET	12.	.	Rest.	BETHUNE/19 COMBINED INQUEST.
"	13".	.	Baths and reorganising of Battalion.	LRe.
"	14".	.	Signalling class, bomb classes, Company drill, baths.	LRe.
"	15".	.	Lieut. Colonel Walter Long. D.S.O. came from the Scots Greys and took over Command. Company drill, bomb classes and signalling classes. Gas demonstration.	LRe.
"	16".	.	Inspection by the G.O.C. Brigade of the Battalion and the transport by the J.B. Divisional Train. Hd. Q. Ft. 19th Division recomposed. G.O.C. Brigade.	LRe.
"	17".	.	Company instruction and inspections.	LRe.
"	18".	.	Bomb throwing & company drill.	LRe.
"	19".	.	The 58th Brigade took over from the 57th Brigade in the forward line. The Battalion moved back to PENIN MARRIAGE. "D" Coy of the 10th Welch was attached to the Battalion for instruction.	LRe.
PENIN MARRIAGE	"	.		
"	20".	.	Bombing aeroplane. Night alarm practiced. Cross country routes to forward line reconnoitred.	LRe.
"	21".	.	Wet rainy day. Bombing instruction and bombing displays. "D" Coy H. 13th Welch attached to Battalion for instruction.	LRe.
"	22".	.	G.O.C. 19th Division visited the Battalion. Wet rainy day. Bombing, aeroplays and Company work.	LRe.

December 1915.

WAR DIARY
or
INTELLIGENCE SUMMARY
(Erase heading not required.)

Army Form C. 2118

Place	Date Dec.	Hour	Summary of Events and Information	Remarks and references to Appendices
IN THE TRENCHES	23rd		Battalion relieved 9 Welch in the trenches. A line was held from COPSE STREET on the right and the LA BASSEE ROAD on the left. "B" & "D" Company in the firing line, "A" in support & "C" Coy in reserve.	BETHUNE CONTOURED SHEET. KRR.
"	24th		A quiet day. A good deal of shell fire by our own artillery. Work done on front line parapet. Work was carried on on new aid post and much attention was paid to local drainage.	KRR.
"	25th		Christmas day. Work done on parapets. "C" Coy relieved "B" Coy in firing line & "A" relieved "D" Coy. Enemy very quiet as usual. C.Q.M.S. MERRITT was instantaneously killed whilst unloading rations from the trolley track by a stray bang.	KRR.
"	26th		Quiet day. Work done on parapets. Working parties from 9 Welch morning and evening.	KRR.
"	27th		Battalion was relieved by 9 Welch - relief completed at 12.15am on 28th Casualties for 23rd, 24th, 25th, 26th, 27th were 1 killed, 1 wounded & 2 self inflicted wounds.	KRR.
CROIX BARBEE	28th		Working party of 60 men found on the firing line. Day spent in cleaning up. Bombing practise &bath.	KRR.
"	29th		"D" Coy Headquarters & 16 Welch attached to Battalion vice 13th Welch. Bomb practise started.	KRR.

December 1915 Sheet No. 3.

Army Form C. 2118

WAR DIARY
or
INTELLIGENCE SUMMARY
(Erase heading not required.)

Instructions regarding War Diaries and Intelligence Summaries are contained in F. S. Regs., Part II. and the Staff Manual respectively. Title Pages will be prepared in manuscript.

Place	Date Dec	Hour	Summary of Events and Information	Remarks and references to Appendices
CROIX BARBEE	30th		Bombing practice. Working parties. Cl. Gibbs arrived.	BETHUNE by COMBINED SHEET 18G.
	31st		Battalion relieved the 9th Welch in the trenches holding the line from Cross St to the LA BASSEE ROAD, "C" "A" on the firing line, "D" in support and "B" in Reserve.	
			The total Casualties 16/31/12/15 are 4 officers killed, 5 wounded and 1 died from wounds received - other ranks, 40 killed, 1 accidentally killed 10 missing, 126 wounded, 5 accidentally wounded and 19 died from wounds.	

Walter Long Lt Col.
6' Batt Wiltshire Regiment

December 1915 - Sheet No 4.

Confidential

War Diary

of

6th (S) Bn Wiltshire Regt.

From 1st January to 31st January 1916.

Volume No 7

WAR DIARY
or
INTELLIGENCE SUMMARY

(Erase heading not required.)

Army Form C. 2118

Instructions regarding War Diaries and Intelligence Summaries are contained in F. S. Regs., Part II and the Staff Manual respectively. Title Pages will be prepared in manuscript.

Place	Date	Hour	Summary of Events and Information	Remarks and references to Appendices
IN THE TRENCHES.	Jany 1916 1st		A very quiet day. A good deal of work done to parapet and Reserve Line.	BETHUNE COMBINED LM SHEET
Do	2nd		Another quiet day. Useful patrol work done by Lt. Trueman and Regimental scouts. Assistance by working parties from 9th Welch made great improvement on the line.	RR
"	3rd		A quiet day. Weather very fine. Lt. Trueman assisted by the scouts fired rifle grenades with effect at the German working parties and machine guns.	LBQ "
"	4th		Battalion relieved by 8th Gloucesters and went into billets at Enguin Road - LE TOURET.	LBQ "
LE TOURET	5th		Baths and refitting. A draft of 102 received comprising men from 1st, 2nd, 3rd & 5th Battalions.	TRQ "
"	6th		Grenade throwing & baths.	LBQ "
"	7th & 8th		Company training. Bomb throwing.	LBQ "
"	9th		G.O.C. inspected the new draft. Church Parade for "B" & "C" Companies.	LBQ "

JANUARY 1916 SHEET No 1.

WAR DIARY
or
INTELLIGENCE SUMMARY
(Erase heading not required.)

Army Form C. 2118

Instructions regarding War Diaries and Intelligence Summaries are contained in F.S. Regs., Part II. and the Staff Manual respectively. Title Pages will be prepared in manuscript.

Place	Date Jan.	Hour	Summary of Events and Information	Remarks and references to Appendices
LE TOURET	10, 11, 12, 13		Company draining - bank throwing hatho.	BETHUNE LRA COMBINED SHEET. LRA
"	14"		Battalion relieved 13" R.W.F. in Reserve at Kings Road.	LRA Do.
"	15"		Working party of 300 men found by Battalion for drainage work.	LRA Do.
"	16"		Sunday - working party found as on previous day.	LRA
"	17"		Working party again found for drainage.	LRA Do.
"	18"		Battalion relieved 9th Welch Regiment in the trenches and held the line RUE de CAILLOUX to FARM CORNER - 1 Company 140 men in the firing line, 1 Company in support, 1 Company at RUE de BERCEAUX and 1 Company less 40 men in Reserve. Capt Allen was wounded.	LRA Do.
IN THE TRENCHES	19"			LRA Do.
"	20, 21, 22		Owing to the fine weather & very light nights a good deal of work was put into the firing line. Very useful work was done by the Regimental Scouts under Lieut. Dytam. Unfortunately L/C Blower was killed whilst on patrol.	LRA Do. LRA Do.
LE TOURET.	29"		Battalion was relieved by 18th + 16th WELCH and went into Billets at Enfatross Road. LE TOURET.	LRA Do.

JANUARY SHEET No. 2.

WAR DIARY
or
INTELLIGENCE SUMMARY
(Erase heading not required.)

Army Form C. 2118

Place	Date	Hour	Summary of Events and Information	Remarks and references to Appendices
LE SART	Jany 24th		Day spent in cleaning up & refitting.	MAP SHEET No 36?
	25th		Battalion moved into fresh billets at LE SART.	224
"	26th 27th		Company drill. Inspection of transport by Commanding Officer on 27th	224 Do.
"	28th 29th		Instruction of M.G. Co by Staff Sergt. from Guards Division - Company training.	224 Do.
"	30.		Church Parade. A draft of 90 men arrived from the 8th Battn.	224 Do.
"	31.		Company training &c.	224 Do.

Walker Lt.Col.

Comdg. 6th (S) Battn. Wiltshire Regt.

JANUARY - SHEET No 3.

Confidential

War Diary
— of —
6th Bn. Wiltshire Regiment.

From 1st February 1916 to 29th February 1916.

Volume No. 8

WAR DIARY
or
INTELLIGENCE SUMMARY

(Erase heading not required.)

Army Form C. 2118

Instructions regarding War Diaries and Intelligence Summaries are contained in F.S. Regs., Part II. and the Staff Manual respectively. Title Pages will be prepared in manuscript.

Place	Date Feby. 1916.	Hour	Summary of Events and Information	Remarks and references to Appendices
LE SART.	1.	—	Company drill, bombing, Arms drill, route marching, signalling instruction	MAP SHEET 36A.
"	2.	—	Company drill, bombing, Arms drill, route marching, signalling instruction. Lecture for Officers by G.O.C. 58 Brigade on discipline.	36A.
"	3 & 4	—	Company drill, bombing, Arms drill, signalling instruction. On the 9th 4"75 fired one practice on the Divisional rifle range, on the 4th 5.5." also fired one practice on the range.	Do 36A.
"	5.	—	Bathing and Company drill - bombing. Several Scheme for Battn. H.Q. and Signallers.	36A. Do
"	6.	—	Sunday – Church Parade – inspection of billets.	36A. Do
"	7. 8. 9. 10.	—	Company drill, bombing, lectured order drill.	36A.
"	11.	—	Company drill. Instruction for N.C.O's. Bombing practice with live bombs. Inter Company Football Tournament 'C' Coy wins. Capt Smith & Trent Gartside joined Battn. 8th Feb 16. Inspection by Lord Kitchener, accompanied by General Hymns and Prince Arthur of Connaught.	36A. Do 36A.
"	12.	—	Company training. Baths. Beat 4th Kings Liverpools 1-0 at Football.	Do 36A.
"	13.	—	Church Parade	36A.

February 1916. SHEET No. 1.

WAR DIARY
or
INTELLIGENCE SUMMARY
(Erase heading not required.)

Army Form C. 2118

Instructions regarding War Diaries and Intelligence Summaries are contained in F.S. Regs., Part II and the Staff Manual respectively. Title Pages will be prepared in manuscript.

Place	Date	Hour	Summary of Events and Information	Remarks and references to Appendices
LE SART	14th	-	Machine Gun Section returned to the Battalion. Company training.	MAP SHEET App. 36A
"	15th	-	Company training. Lieuts Tayland & Tynan proceeded to Canadian Division for instruction in Bombing.	App.
PONT DU HEM.	16th	-	19th Divn relieved guards Divn. Brigade moved up to Jerung Line. Battn moved to Billets at PONT DUHEM. Very wet & windy day.	App.
"	17th	-	Company drill. Officers Inspection of new line of Trenches.	App.
IN THE TRENCHES	18th	-	Battn relieved 9th Welch Regt holding Line from MOATED GRANGE to ERITH ROAD. 'A' Coy Right Front. 'B' Coy Centre. 'D' Left Front. 'C' Coy holding Posts. Pte Hunt Killed	App.
"	19th	-	Quiet day. Manual repairs to parapets. L/Sgt Durrant wounded	App.
PONT DU HEM	20th	-	Bright & Sunny day. Battn relieved by 9th Welch Regt & returned to Billets at PONT DU HEM.	App.
"	21st	-	Good day. Wire drill & Company drill	App.

FEBRUARY. 1916. SHEET No 2.

WAR DIARY
or
INTELLIGENCE SUMMARY
(Erase heading not required.)

Army Form C. 2118

Instructions regarding War Diaries and Intelligence Summaries are contained in F. S. Regs., Part II. and the Staff Manual respectively. Title Pages will be prepared in manuscript.

Place	Date	Hour	Summary of Events and Information	Remarks and references to Appendices
IN THE TRENCHES.	22	—	Snowed hard. Relieved 9th Welsh Regt in the firing line. Kent Bantridge joined Battn.	MAP SHEET SR 36A
"	23	—	More snow which hindered work and patrols. Reforms to front line were. C.S.M. Butler killed.	KR4 "
LA GORGUE	24	—	Relieved by 10 Worcester Regt and marched to Billets at LA GORGUE. Billets near the Church.	KR4 "
"	25	—	General cleaning up. Very cold & frosty day. Lieut Layland Lyman returned from attachment to the Canadians.	KR4 "
"	26	—	Owing to a very heavy fall of snow drill was rather hindered. However bombing was practised and the Battalion had baths at LA GORGUE.	KR4 "
"	27	—	Sunday - Church Parade.	KR4 "
"	28	—	Company drill - working party sent to PONT DU HEM to work on SOUTH TILLEROY TRENCH.	KR4 "
"	29	—	Battalion again went to Baths - Bombing practice - Machine gun	KR4 "

FEBRUARY 1916 Sheet No 3

WAR DIARY
or
INTELLIGENCE SUMMARY

(Erase heading not required.)

Army Form C. 2118

Instructions regarding War Diaries and Intelligence Summaries are contained in F. S. Regs., Part II. and the Staff Manual respectively. Title Pages will be prepared in manuscript.

Place	Date Feby	Hour	Summary of Events and Information	Remarks and references to Appendices
LA GORGUE	29.		instructors for Company machine gunners. During the stay at LA GORGUE Company signallers were also trained. Casualties for this month were, Officers Nil, other ranks - 2 killed and 2 wounded. 1 Officer & 24 other ranks admitted to Hospital Sick. Strength of Battalion to this date - 36 Officers and 874 other ranks. H.B. Hartley Major Comm'g 6th Wiltshire Regt.	MAP SHEET 36 A. Loos

FEBRUARY 1916. SHEET No 4.

6" Wilts
Vol 9

Confidential.

War diary
— of —

6th (Service) Bn Wiltshire Regiment.

From 1st March 1916 to 31st March 1916.

Volume 9.

WAR DIARY or INTELLIGENCE SUMMARY

Army Form C. 2118

Place	Date MARCH 1916	Hour	Summary of Events and Information	Remarks and references to Appendices
IN THE TRENCHES.	1.	—	The Brigade went into the firing line from COPSE STREET to KINKROO KEEP - The Battalion occupying the trenches from FARM CORNER to KINKROO with the Cheshires on their left. "A" & "C" Companies were in the firing line and "D" Company in support, "B" Company in Reserve. One Company of the 20th Lancs Fusiliers was attached to the Battalion for instruction.	MAP SHEET BETHUNE COMBINED. LBQ.
Do.	2	—	A bright fine day - an extensive amount of work done both on firing line and old British line. The trenches were left in a bad condition by the previous Brigade which took a considerable amount of time to clean up. The right fire Company ("A" Company) were shelled during the afternoon but suffered no casualties. In the evening patrols reported german working parties which were fired on by our artillery with what is thought to be with successful result. Working parties from the Pioneers Pioneers and the R.E.'s were sent to assist in building up the firing line parapet and continuing the old earthwork.	Do. LRQ1
Do.	3	—	Very showery day. 2 men of the left Company were sniped early in the morning. Enemy sent about fifteen 5.9 shells in the vicinity of Battalion Headquarters barricade house.	LQQ.
Do.	4	—	Owing to the inclement weather the Battalion was relieved by the 9th Welch and went into Billets at KINGS ROAD.	LRQp.

MARCH 1916 - Sheet No. 1.

Army Form C. 2118

WAR DIARY
or
INTELLIGENCE SUMMARY
(Erase heading not required.)

Instructions regarding War Diaries and Intelligence Summaries are contained in F. S. Regs., Part II. and the Staff Manual respectively. Title Pages will be prepared in manuscript.

Place	Date MARCH	Hour	Summary of Events and Information	Remarks and references to Appendices
RUE DES CHEVATTE.	1916. 5th		A bright and sunny day. Time was spent in general cleaning up. Two working parties of 50 Men each required carrying up R.E. material to TUBE STATION in the evening.	BETHUNE COMBINED SHEET. 1.A.a
Do.	6th		Neual Company inoculation. 2 Working Parties required on ROPE TRENCH in the evening.	1.A.b.
Do.	7th		Battalion was relieved by 18th Lancs Fusiliers and went into billets at PARADIS. Heavy snow fell at night.	1.A.c. 1.A.d.
PARADIS.	8th		Battalion went to baths at LA GORGUE.	
Do.	9th		Company drill, Classes for machine gunners, N.C.O's & signallers. Remainder of Battalion had baths at LA GORGUE.	1.A.e. Do. 1.A.f.
Do.	10th		A draft of 78 Men from the 3rd & 8th Battalions arrived.	1.A.g. Do.
Do.	11th		Bombing practice. Classes of instruction - Company Drill.	1.A.h.
Do.	12th		A considerable change in the weather - since fine day. Church Parade.	1.A.i.
Do.	13th		Company Training - bomb throwing - Classes of Instruction.	1.A.j.

MARCH. 1916 - Sheet No. 2.

WAR DIARY
or
INTELLIGENCE SUMMARY

(Erase heading not required.)

Army Form C. 2118

Instructions regarding War Diaries and Intelligence Summaries are contained in F. S. Regs., Part II. and the Staff Manual respectively. Title Pages will be prepared in manuscript.

Place	Date 1916	Hour	Summary of Events and Information	Remarks and references to Appendices
PARADIS	MARCH 14	—	Battalion moved to billets at CROIX BARBEE taking over the PENIN MARRIAGE Billets from the 56th Brigade. 80 men had to be employed on "B" line during the day near RICHEBOURG ST VAAST. 2 parties of 60 men carrying on with the work on RUE DE BOIS near NEUVE CHAPELLE. 3 parties of 50 men each carrying R.E. material in the evening.	BETHUNE COMBINED SHEET. L.R.9
CROIX BARBEE	15	—	2 working parties of 80 each under Lieut. Mortimer completed the wiring scheme on the RUE DE BOIS near NEUVE CHAPELLE by night. 3 Working parties of 50 men each carrying R.E. material from EUSTON POST.	L.R.9
"	16	—	2 Working parties of 50 men each carrying R.E. material from EUSTON POST.	L.R.9
"	17	—	2 Working parties by day of 25 men each and worked on "B" Reserve Line. Battalion relieved 9th Welch in the firing line – "D" Company taking over from LIVERPOOL ST to HUN STREET – "B" Company from HUN STREET to LA BASSEE ROAD – "C" Company LA BASSEE RD to HUN STREET – "D" Company held HILL'S Redoubt – "A" Company PORT ARTHUR KEEP & LANSDOWNE POST with one platoon in each and 3 platoons in Reserve.	L.R.9

Sheet No. 3. MARCH 1916.

WAR DIARY
or
INTELLIGENCE SUMMARY
(Erase heading not required.)

Army Form. C. 2118

Instructions regarding War Diaries and Intelligence Summaries are contained in F. S. Regs, Part II. and the Staff Manual respectively. Title Pages will be prepared in manuscript.

Place	Date MARCH	Hour	Summary of Events and Information	Remarks and references to Appendices
IN THE TRENCHES.	1916. 18 } 19. } 20. }		3 Very good days as regards weather. Battalion was comfortable as regards casualties PRIVATES HUNT, WOOD, & KING being killed. A great deal of work was done on firing line. Headquarters and PORT ARTHUR Redoubt. Leave re-opened on the 19?.	MAP SHEET 36A LDA.
	21.		Enemy bombarded NEUVE CHAPELLE for 2 an hour This however did not cause any casualties to the Battalion or destroy their line. Battalion relieved by 9? WELCH and went back to billets at CROIX BARBEE.	LDA
CROIX BARBEE.	22.		Working parties carrying R.E. material all night. Baths during the day.	" LDA
DO.	23.		Battalion relieved by 7. East Lancs. and marched to billets at REGNIER de CLERC near MERVILLE.	LDA
MERVILLE	24		Bitterly cold day - snowing. Battalion had baths & boots fitted.	LDA
"	25		Battalion made an early start - leaving MERVILLE at 8am and went into billets in KINGS ROAD.	LDA
KINGS ROAD	26		Sunday.	LDA
RUE DES CHAVATTE.	27		The Battalion took over line at TUBE STATION from 9? WELCH - "A" &	LDA

MARCH 1916 - Reel No 4.

WAR DIARY
or
INTELLIGENCE SUMMARY
(Erase heading not required.)

Army Form C. 2118

Place	Date	Hour	Summary of Events and Information	Remarks and references to Appendices
IN THE TRENCHES.	28 29 30 31		In the firing line & B v D in Reserve. First 2 days very windy weather. Little work could be done but weather improved a great deal and much work was done during the next 2 days. D Coy relieved "D" Company in the firing line on night of 29/30. One casualty, one 3 men wounded on the Look out. On 31st Battalion went back to billets in King's road on relief by 9 Welsh. During this four days Lt Tynan did useful work patrolling.	MAP SHEET L N J 36 A " " "

Walker Ing

Lt Col

Comdg. 6th (S) Battn, Wiltshire Regt.

MARCH 1916 Sheet No 5

6 Wilts
Vol 10

~~XX~~

Confidential

War Diary
— of —
6th (Service) Bn Wiltshire Regiment.

From 1st April 1916 to 30th April 1916.

Volume 10.

WAR DIARY
or
INTELLIGENCE SUMMARY

(Erase heading not required.)

Army Form C. 2118

Instructions regarding War Diaries and Intelligence Summaries are contained in F. S. Regs., Part II. and the Staff Manual respectively. Title Pages will be prepared in manuscript.

Place	Date April 1916	Hour	Summary of Events and Information	Remarks and references to Appendices
RUE DES CAVATIES	1.		A lovely warm day. 2nd Lt Hoskins went to Field Ambulance Sick. Battalion had baths and boot fitting - cleaning up billets.	MAP SHEET 36A. EpHK. PHK.
Do.	2		Sunday.	
Do.	3.		Very hot day - usual Company instruction - working party found at night carrying R.E. material to TUBE STATION.	EpHK
Do.	4.		Battalion relieved 9" Welch and took over line at TUBE STATION.	EpHK
IN THE TRENCHES	5.		Enemy were very quiet - a good deal of work was done both on firing line and on British line. One man wounded.	EpHK
Do.	6		Work continued on parapets - enemy quiet. Capt Leroy went to Hospital sick.	EpHK
Do.	7.		Battalion Headquarters - barricade house heavily shelled in the afternoon. One man (a signaller) was killed and 2 wounded. Headquarters had to be evacuated until the shelling ceased, which shelling lasted for about an hour. Work continued on improving firing line.	EpHK
Do.	8		Headquarters were again heavily shelled but fortunately there were no casualties. Battalion was relieved by 9" Welch in the evening	EpHK

WAR DIARY
or
INTELLIGENCE SUMMARY

(Erase heading not required.)

Army Form C. 2118

Instructions regarding War Diaries and Intelligence Summaries are contained in F. S. Regs., Part II. and the Staff Manual respectively. Title Pages will be prepared in manuscript.

Place	Date	Hour	Summary of Events and Information	Remarks and references to Appendices
			and went back to billets at KINGS ROAD - A party of 100 men left behind to work on dugouts. Lt. Dynam & scouts also reconnoitred behind with the object of capturing a German listening post. Lt. Dynam went on between the lines and got between the German lines & their listening post. When he got within a few yards from post, he ordered the occupants to "hands up" and was met with a burst which fortunately failed to explode. Lt. Dynam retaliated with about with the scout that 2 Germans were killed whilst a third ran away & walked into our lines.	MAP SHEET 36A
KINGS ROAD RUE DES CHAVATTES	9"		Day spent in general cleaning up - Battalion had baths and took photos. Working party of 250 men found at night. Covering R.E. material. Capt. Smith went to hospital sick.	G.O.H.C.
Do	10"		Baths - Mens & Company inspection - Working party found as on previous day.	G.O.H.C.
Do	11"		Lt. Dynam and scouts went out from 9° utter limits on patrol. Whilst proceeding along to the German lines, he came across an enemy patrol which with he and his scouts - very cleverly surrounded and ordered them to surrender. This they did	G.O.H.C.

1875 Wt. W593/826 1,000,000 4/15 J.B.C. & A. A.D.S.S./Forms/C. 2118.

WAR DIARY or INTELLIGENCE SUMMARY

Army Form C. 2118

Instructions regarding War Diaries and Intelligence Summaries are contained in F.S. Regs., Part II. and the Staff Manual respectively. Title Pages will be prepared in manuscript.

(Erase heading not required.)

Place	Date	Hour	Summary of Events and Information	Remarks and references to Appendices
RUE DES CHAVATTES			and the patrol which consisted of an officer, a sergeant and a private were taken prisoners	MAP SHEET 36 A
Do	12"		Battalion again had baths and a working party was found in the evening as on previous day.	G.O.H.
Do			Battalion relieved 9th Welch on the trenches taking over the line at TUBE STATION. One man Machine gunner was killed.	G.O.H.
IN THE TRENCHES	13"		Enemy more active than usual. Lt Williams did useful work while on patrol. Snipers thicker and some sniping done.	G.O.H.
	14"		Enemy fire was heavily interchanged – enemy very active with machine guns. Another man was unfortunately killed. Lt Williams and scouts went out on patrol but owing to the brightness of the moon very little reconnaissance was done.	G.O.H.
Do	15"		Very quiet day. Work continued improving trenches	
Do	16"		Sunday. Battalion was relieved by 9 Welch Regt & proceeded to Rocane Billets at KINGS Road. Leaving the morning Battalion Headquarters – Farmhouse North was slightly shelled but there were no casualties. Several dugouts were made during the four days in the Trenches.	G.O.H.
RUE DES CHAVATTES	17"		Day spent in cleaning up billets – bath, boot fitting.	G.O.H.

1875 Wt. W593/826 1,000,000 4/15 J.B.C.&A. A.D.S.S./Forms/C.2118.

WAR DIARY
or
INTELLIGENCE SUMMARY
(Erase heading not required.)

Army Form C. 2118

Instructions regarding War Diaries and Intelligence Summaries are contained in F. S. Regs., Part II. and the Staff Manual respectively. Title Pages will be prepared in manuscript.

Place	Date April	Hour	Summary of Events and Information	Remarks and references to Appendices
KINGS RD RUE DES CHAVATTES	18		News was received that 2nd Lt. Groom had been awarded the Distinguished Service Order. Usual Company instruction.	MAP SHEET 36A.
Do	19		Battalion was relieved by 1st Gloucester Regt. and proceeded to billets at LES LOBES - reaching my Tent (sub Warnery)	Do.
LES LOBES.	20.		Battalion made an early start and proceeded to ROBECQ taking over billets from 10th Warwick Regiment, arriving there at about 12/30 p.m. - remainder of day spent in cleaning up billets.	Do.
ROBECQ.	21.		Good Friday - Church Parade.	HAZEBROUCQ. 5A.
Do.	22.		Battalion moved away from ROBECQ this day and meeting remainder of Brigade at LA MIQUELLERIE proceeded to QUERNES for the purpose of training. Reached new billets at about 4/30 p.m. Wet and cold day.	Do.
QUERNES.	23.		Sunday - resting and cleaning up of billets.	Do.
Do	24		Company training - Machine gun instruction - signalling & bombing.	Do.
Do	25		Training as on previous day.	Do.

WAR DIARY
or
INTELLIGENCE SUMMARY
(Erase heading not required.)

Army Form C. 2118

Instructions regarding War Diaries and Intelligence Summaries are contained in F. S. Regs., Part II. and the Staff Manual respectively. Title Pages will be prepared in manuscript.

Place	Date April	Hour	Summary of Events and Information	Remarks and references to Appendices
QUERNES	26.		Training as on previous 2 days.	MAP SHEET HAZEBROUCK 5A.
Do.	27.		Do.	
Do.	28.		Battalion training – Lecture to Stretcher bearers by Medical Officer.	
Do.	29.		Battalion training – Scheme between A & B Companies versus C & D Companies. A "18" under Capt. Stares and C & D under Major Hartley. Stretcher bearers carried as on previous day.	
Do.	30.		Battalion training – forming bombing squads and action in trenches.	Do.

50 N.C.Os.

Wallsdre
Lt. Col.
Commanding 6th Leicestershire Regt.

6 Wilts
Vol 11

Confidential

War Diary
of
6th (S) Bn Wiltshire Regiment.

From 1st May 1916 to 31st May 1916.

Volume 11.

From
    Officer Commanding
    6th Bn Wiltshire Regt

To
    D.A.G.
    3rd Echelon

Herewith War Diary for May 1916 (Volume II) in accordance with G.R.O. 1598 of 30th May 1916.

L B Grey

In the Field
1/6/1916
                    Lt-Col
            Commndg 6th Bn Wiltshire Regt.

WAR DIARY
or
INTELLIGENCE SUMMARY
(Erase heading not required.)

Army Form C. 2118

Instructions regarding War Diaries and Intelligence Summaries are contained in F. S. Regs., Part II. and the Staff Manual respectively. Title Pages will be prepared in manuscript.

Place	Date 1916 May	Hour	Summary of Events and Information	Remarks and references to Appendices
QUERNES	1st	-	Battalion Training.	MAP SHEET MAZE DROUT 5A
"	2 } 3	-	Brigade Field days at FLEUCETTE.	LR4
"	4	-	Divisional Field day. Division attacked ENGUINGATTE – Sir Douglas Haig was present.	LR4.
"	5	-	Divisional Signalling Scheme at ENGUINGATTE – Platoon training by remainder of Battalion.	LR4.
"	6	-	Platoon training.	LR4
"	7	-	Left QUERNES at 11am and entrained at BERGUETTE leaving at 2pm.	LR4
"	8	-	Arrived at LONGEAU near AMIENS at 10/30 p.m. Marched to FLESSELLES arriving at about 5 a/c on morning of 8th. 2nd Lt. R.C. WHITE arrived on 7th.	
FLESSELLES	9 10 11 12 13	- - - - -	Platoon training consisting of arm and squad drill – route marching in particular – bombing and consolidation of trenches after an attack – also machine gun signalling classes. Afternoons spent in footballing, sports and boxing. Draft of 15 Men arrived on the 12th.	MAP SHEET JENS 11 1 Pg.
"	14	-	Sunday	1 Pg.

1875 Wt. W593/826 1,000,000 4/15 J.B.C. & A. A.D.S.S./Form/C. 2118.

WAR DIARY
or
INTELLIGENCE SUMMARY

(Erase heading not required.)

Army Form C. 2118

Instructions regarding War Diaries and Intelligence Summaries are contained in F. S. Regs, Part II. and the Staff Manual respectively. Title Pages will be prepared in manuscript.

Place	Date	Hour	Summary of Events and Information	Remarks and references to Appendices
FLESSELLES	15		Platoon training - Special importance being given to training of Platoon Commanders. Attacking and consolidating trenches. Bombing. Period revising. Class for N.C.O's under regimental Sergt. Major. Training of reserve machine gunners and signallers. In the afternoons regimental Sports, shooting contests.	MAP SHEET LENS 11.
	16			186
	17			
	18			
	19			
	20			184.
	21.		Sunday - Church Parade.	
	22.		Platoon training. Attacking and consolidating trenches. night bombing. Period revising. Class of instruction for N.C.O's under Regimental Sergt. Major. Training of reserve machine gunners & signallers. Afternoons devoted to training & competitions for Brigade & Divisional Sports.	184.
	23			
	24			
	25			1841
	26.		Platoon Training. Brigade Sports in the afternoon. and bayonet Battalion won the bombing assault - second in the storage race. the digging competition & Lewis Gun Race.	184
	27.		Platoon training. Divisional Sports in the afternoon. Battalion did first in bombing assault competition.	184
	28.		Sunday - Church Parade.	
	29		Left FLESSELLES at 7am and with remainder of 58th Brigade marched	184/

Army Form C. 2118

WAR DIARY
or
INTELLIGENCE SUMMARY

(Erase heading not required.)

Instructions regarding War Diaries and Intelligence Summaries are contained in F. S. Regs., Part II. and the Staff Manual respectively. Title Pages will be prepared in manuscript.

Place	Date	Hour	Summary of Events and Information	Remarks and references to Appendices
GORENFLOS	30th		To GORENFLOS arriving at 12 noon.	MAP SHEET LENS. 11.
			Brigade continued its march and arrived at MILLANCOURT at 11 am.	124
MILLANCOURT	31st		Work in our Station Commanders - reconnaissance of ST. RIQUIER training area.	124
	31/5/16			

Walker
Lt Col.
Comdg. 6th (S) Battn, Wiltshire Regt.

6 wilts June
VOL 12

XIX

Confidential

War diary
— of —
6ᵗʰ Bⁿ Wiltshire Regiment

From 1ˢᵗ June 1916 — to — 30ᵗʰ June 1916.

Volume 12.

WAR DIARY
or
INTELLIGENCE SUMMARY
(Erase heading not required.)

Army Form C. 2118

Instructions regarding War Diaries and Intelligence Summaries are contained in F. S. Regs., Part II. and the Staff Manual respectively. Title Pages will be prepared in manuscript.

Place	Date 1916	Hour	Summary of Events and Information	Remarks and references to Appendices
MILLENCOURT	June 1		Battalion training - attack practice and consolidation.	LM4 NORTH WEST EUROPE SHEET 1 & 2 now out of 4.
"	" 2		Brigade training - attack practice on imaginary German Line.	LM4
"	" 3		Battalion training - attack and consolidation of position. Lance Cpl. Ford awarded G.C.M. - Capt. Tunnell and "Scout Weam" awarded Military Medals.	LM4
"	" 4		Sunday - Church Parade.	LM4
"	" 5		Brigade training - Battalion carried out same scheme as on 2nd instant.	LM4
"	" 6		Brigade training - Battalion represented enemy on this day in attack by 57th Brigade.	LM4
"	" 7		Brigade attack - advancing in smoke helmets. 2nd Lieuts. J.a.C. Wood, Barrett & Hannam arrived.	LM4
"	" 8		Battalion route march - 2nd Lieuts. Williams, Brick, Stopson & Weir joined Battalion.	LM4
"	" 9		Divisional day. G.O.C. Fourth Army was present. Battalion attacked and consolidated German 2nd Line position.	LM4 LENS SHEET 11 & AMIENS 12
"	" 10		Battalion marched to fresh billets at GORENFLOS staying here for the night.	LM4
GORENFLOS	" 11		Battalion marched to ST VAST.	LM4
ST VAST	" 12		6th day. Company training. Bombing and Machine Gun instruction.	LM4
"	" 13		Baton training - Battalion attended a memorial service for Lord Kitchener which was held at TRONCOURT.	LM4
"	" 14		Battalion left ST VAST and proceeded to RAINNEVILLE staying there the night.	LM4
RAINNEVILLE	" 15		Battalion made an early start and proceeded to camp W. of ALBERT. The enemy fired four shells soon after arrival into our camp.	LM4
ALBERT	" 16		Major Lord Tynne from the Worcester Regiment arrived to take over Second in Command. Working parties found at night.	LENS SHEET 11 LM4 BM4 LM4
"	" 17		These days were spent in getting Battalion thoroughly equipped. Working parties	
"	" 18		found at night.	

1875 Wt. W.593/826 1,000,000 4/15 J.B.C. & A. A.D.S.S./Forms/C. 2118.

WAR DIARY
or
INTELLIGENCE SUMMARY

(Erase heading not required.)

Army Form C. 2118

Instructions regarding War Diaries and Intelligence Summaries are contained in F. S. Regs., Part II. and the Staff Manual respectively. Title Pages will be prepared in manuscript.

Place	Date 1916	Hour	Summary of Events and Information	Remarks and references to Appendices
ALBERT.	June 19		A draft of 104 other ranks joined Battalion. - Working parties as on previous nights.	Appx "Lens" 11
"	" 20		1871 and using days - Training at intervals - digging points at night.	104 "
"	" 21			
"	" 22			
"	" 23		Our artillery very active during these days - mostly hanging. - Working parties at	104 "
"	" 24		night. Capt. de Launay arrived on 25th.	
"	" 25			
"	" 26			
"	" 27		Commanding Officer's inspection of Battalion in fighting order.	104 "
"	" 28		Rest all day. Operations postponed for 48 hours.	104 "
"	" 29		Finishing off preparations - inspections etc.	104 "
"	" 30		All packs &c sent back to Divisional train - Battalion moved at 10pm to preliminary position south of new Bridge on the railway line at ALBERT.	194 "

Wall Ing Lt Col.
Commdg 6th Wiltshire Regiment.

58th Inf.Bde.
19th Div.

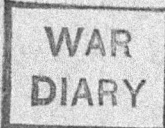

6th BATTN. THE WILTSHIRE REGIMENT.

J U L Y

1 9 1 6

56/13

Vol 13

877c
SD

Confidential

War Diary
of
6"/19" Wiltshire Regt

From 1st June 1916 to 31st July 1916

Volume - 13.

WAR DIARY or INTELLIGENCE SUMMARY

(Erase heading not required.)

Army Form C. 2118

Instructions regarding War Diaries and Intelligence Summaries are contained in F. S. Regs., Part II. and the Staff Manual respectively. Title Pages will be prepared in manuscript.

Place	Date 1916	Hour	Summary of Events and Information	Remarks and references to Appendices
ALBERT	July 1	—	At 7.30am Brigade moved up to position on TARA USNA trenches - Orders were received to attack LA BOISELLE from the South during that night which however did not take place.	ALBERT COMBINED SHEET. LMC
"	" 2.		At 9.30pm orders were received to take up position in front line at 11pm. At 11pm Battalion advanced in open order and attacked German front line system of trenches just South of LA BOISELLE. Two lines of trenches were taken and consolidated. Cheshires were on our right flank and Welch Fusiliers on our left. Our losses were Lt-Colonel Lt. Allen, King & Bigg killed - Capt Tanner, Lis Speight, Reed, Lyran Capt Henry (RAMC) wounded. Other ranks were 35 killed, 237 wounded and 35 missing. The night was spent in consolidating - no counter attack was made by the enemy.	LMC
"	" 3.		Brigade attacked LA BOISELLE from the North and carried it. In conformity with the attack Battalion advanced from the communication trenches due East lies owing to 57th Brigade being driven back we were compelled to withdraw to our consolidated position. Battalion was relieved this night by 56th Brigade with exception of 150 men.	Beq
"	" 4.		Remainder of Battalion withdrawn from the line.	JM

WAR DIARY or INTELLIGENCE SUMMARY

Army Form C. 2118

Place	Date	Hour	Summary of Events and Information	Remarks and references to Appendices
ALBERT.	July 5 1916		Battalion reorganised.	ALBERT COMBINED (SHEET.)
"	"	7.	Battalion moved at 6am from TARA USNA Line and took up position between HORSE SHOE LANE and HELIGOLAND on the German Front Line opposite. At 8/8.30am Battalion advanced in support of 9th Welch and took up a line conforming with 56th Brigade on LA BOISSELLE - CONTALMAISON Road. 57th Brigade on our right attempted to attack BAILIFF WOOD - CONTALMAISON but were driven back thereby leaving our line on the "air" with a gap of 600 yards. In the afternoon from line suffered casualties from German snipers on our right. These snipers however were killed by our bombers late in the evening. Seeing the night the Durham Light Infantry came on our right and took up the position just North West of BAILIFF Wood. This was taken over in the morning by the Welsh Fusiliers from our Brigade. Our men were in a very exhausted condition. The night was a very wet and trying one but the enemy did not attempt any counter-attack.	184
"	"	8.	Continued consolidating position. The enemy subjected to heavy artillery fire during the day. Late in the afternoon it was thought enemy were going to attempt a counter attack but nothing came of it. It is thought owing to well directed fire on CONTALMAISON by our heavy artillery, the only result being that the enemy retaliated by heavy heavy	

WAR DIARY
or
INTELLIGENCE SUMMARY

(Erase heading not required.)

Army Form C. 2118

Place	Date 1916	Hour	Summary of Events and Information	Remarks and references to Appendices
BAIZIEUX	July 9		Shelling our position and forming a barrage at HELIGOLAND & SAUSAGE VALLEY. During the night and early morning of 9/9 Battalion was relieved by Royal Warwicks Regiment of 112th Brigade. The Battalion went to billets in ALBERT. At 9pm the same evening Battalion moved to billets at BAIZIEUX where a draft of 109 men from the 3rd Battn. arrived.	LRM AMIENS 17
"	" 10		Reorganisation and re-equipping.	LRM
"	" 11		Inspection of new draft.	LRM.
"	" 12		Platoon Training - Draft of 33 men arrived from Hampshire Regiment	LRM
"	" 13		Platoon Training. Class of instruction for Lance Corporals & Corporals	LRM "
"	" 14		under Regimental Sergeant Major.	LRM "
"	" 15		Platoon Training. 2nd Lt. Kenstead arrived.	LRM "
"	" 16		Sunday - Church Parade.	LRM
"	" 17		Platoon Training - Lecture of N.C.O's & Officers by Divisional Commander.	LRM
"	" 18		Platoon Training	LRM "
"	" 19		Platoon Training	LRM

WAR DIARY
or
INTELLIGENCE SUMMARY
(Erase heading not required.)

Army Form C. 2118

Instructions regarding War Diaries and Intelligence Summaries are contained in F. S. Regs., Part II. and the Staff Manual respectively. Title Pages will be prepared in manuscript.

Place	Date July	Hour	Summary of Events and Information	Remarks and references to Appendices
BAIZIEUX	20		Battalion moved from BAIZIEUX to bivouacs at BECOURT WOOD in the afternoon	1/4 M. A/SGT COMBINED SHEET. LRU
BECOURT WOOD	21		Battalion moved this morning from BECOURT WOOD to South end of MAMETZ Wood which was heavily shelled in the afternoon	
MAMETZ	22		After 3 barrages of German fire Battalion changed their position in the wood on the afternoon to further South of the wood. "A" "B" Companies were attached to S.W.B. for the night to dig a support trench but owing to the attack by the 56 Brigade not being successful these Companies were not employed & returned early next morning.	LRU "
"	23		Battalion relieved Loyal North Lancs of 56° Brigade in front line. "D" Company taking up position from S2c71 to S8 b99 - "C" Company from S8a S6 to S8b67 - "B" Company from S8a34 to S8b67 - "A" Company from S8a24 to S8a68 - Headquarters being at S8a63 in a large German dugout. "C" Company dug a trench from S2a30 to S8d69. A quiet night was spent and a considerable amount of wiring was done.	LA4 S2c71 to S8a99.
In the trenches	24		Intermittent shelling by the enemy. A great deal of artillery fire at	

WAR DIARY or INTELLIGENCE SUMMARY

(Erase heading not required.)

Army Form C. 2118

6th Bn Wiltshire Regt   July 1916

Place	Date 1916	Hour	Summary of Events and Information	Remarks and references to Appendices
In the Trenches	July 25.		night and barrages, one at 9pm at night repelling a counter attack from LONGUEVAL which had spread over area occupied by Battalion. Work was not possible until the early hours of the next morning.	ALBERT COMBINED SHEET LRM
"	26.		Bombing attack by enemy reported in progress. "E" Company continued digging trench. Enemy put over barrage over our lines but nothing happened.	LRM
"	27.		A trench was dug by "A" Company from S.2.d.40 and S.2.d.50 Connecting up with the Rebel Trench on their right - "B" Company wiring. "B" Company relieved "D" Company in the firing line -	LRM "
"	27.		Battalion found up 2 barricades - one on BAZENTIN & MAMETZ ROADS and the other on BAZENTIN LE PETIT main street.	LRM
"	28.		Enemy shelled line held by E Company during the afternoon. Heavy barricade continued.	LRM
"	29.		Battalion relieved in trenches by 57th Brigade and marched to bivouac in BECOURT WOOD.	LRM
"	30.		Battalion left BECOURT WOOD at 12noon and marched to	LRM

Army Form C. 2118

WAR DIARY
or
INTELLIGENCE SUMMARY
(Erase heading not required.)

Instructions regarding War Diaries and Intelligence Summaries are contained in F.S. Regs., Part II. and the Staff Manual respectively. Title Pages will be prepared in manuscript.

Place	Date 1916	Hour	Summary of Events and Information	Remarks and references to Appendices
LA HOUSSOYE	July 31		Billets at LA HOUSSOYE - Very hot day which made march very disagreeable.	AMIENS 17
			Day spent in settling the men. Battalion went bathing in a neighbouring stream.	
			From the 2nd instant to 29 instant our casualties were 2 in all ranks. Brown wounded - other ranks 29 wounded + 6 killed.	
	1/8/1916			

P.B. Green
Capt. & Adjt
for Lt Col.
Comg. 6 Bn Wiltshire Regt.

58th Brigade.
19th Division.

1/6th BATTALION

WILTSHIRE REGIMENT

AUGUST 1 9 1 6

Army Form C. 2118

WAR DIARY or INTELLIGENCE SUMMARY
(Erase heading not required.)

Instructions regarding War Diaries and Intelligence Summaries are contained in F.S. Regs., Part II. and the Staff Manual respectively. Title Pages will be prepared in manuscript.

Place	Date 1916 Aug.	Hour	Summary of Events and Information	Remarks and references to Appendices
LA HOUSSOYE.	1st & 2nd	—	Platoon Training – bathing & refitting.	24. LENS
"	3rd	—	Battalion left LA HOUSSOYE and entrained at FRECHENCOURT arriving at LONGPRE STATION at about 8:30pm. Battalion then proceeded to billets at COCQUEREL arriving about 10/15pm.	1/2 Sheet 11.
COCQUEREL	4th	—	Cleaning up billets &c. Platoon Training – Class of Instruction for all N.C.O.'s under Regimental Sergeant Major.	
"	5th	—	Platoon Training – Battalion went bathing in River Somme. Class of Instruction for N.C.O.'s under Regimental Sergeant Major.	AMIENS 1/2 Sheet 12.
"	6th	—	Battalion left COCQUEREL entraining at PONT REMY at about 1pm arriving at BAILLEUL STATION at 11:30pm. Battalion then marched to camp at N17c near KEMMEL.	"
N.KEMMEL	7th	—	Battalion relieved 4th YORKS (50th Division) in the trenches on the SPANBROEKMOLEN and NYTSCHAETE Line taking over from N.15c to about N.24c. "A" & "D" Companies on the firing line – "C" Company in support and "D" in Reserve.	FRANCE and BELGIUM 1/2 Sheet 28 S.W.
On the trenches	8th	—	2nd Lt. Beech & Greene from the Shoreditch Dragoons joined.	"
"	9th 10th & 11th	—	Seeing this has been in the trenches a great deal of work was done owing to the bad condition of the line. On the whole the enemy were very quiet – most afternoons they bombarded our front line with Minenwerfers. The casualties were slight, 1 man being killed and 1 wounded. The damage done to trenches was slight with the exception of breaching our parapet in several places on the afternoon of the 12th. The enemy shelled our front line position with heavy shells this afternoon.	"
"	On the night of 12/13	—	"B" Company relieved "D" on the firing line and "D" Company relieved "C". A draft of 46 other ranks arrived on the 10th.	"
"	13th	—	Battalion relieved by 9th Welch and proceeded to camp on N19a near KEMMEL in Divisional Reserve.	"

August 1916. Sheet 1.

WAR DIARY or INTELLIGENCE SUMMARY

Army Form C. 2118

Place	Date 1916 Augt.	Hour	Summary of Events and Information	Remarks and references to Appendices
Nr. KEMMEL	14th	—	Day spent in general cleaning up and bathing.	FRANCE & BELGIUM Sheet 28 S.W.
"	15.16.17 & 18th		Minor training – bathing – Class of instruction under Regimental Sergeant Major for all N.C.O.'s. Lt. Col. Osman Rea joined on 15th. 2 days of bivouac tanks joined on 18th. N.19.a.	N.19.a.
"	19th		Battalion relieved 9th Welch in the trenches taking over line from N.18.c. to about N.24.c. "C" & "D" Companies on the firing line – "B" on Reserve & "A" in support.	
"	20.21		Night of 20/21 "B" Company relieved "C" and "D" relieved "D" – "C" Company going into Reserve – "D" Company into support. Afternoons of 21st and 22nd front line bombarded by Minenwerfers. Rifle grenades fired at night – our method of retaliation satisfactory. Casualties during this period were 1 killed and 6 wounded.	FRANCE & BELGIUM Sheet 28 S.W. N.18.c – N.24.c.
"	22.23 24&25		On the 21st 2/Lt. G.N. Atkinson joined, coming south from a draft of 20 other ranks. Capt.& R. Gillow & Lieut. G.H. Cox arrived on the 22nd. Night of 25/26 Battalion was relieved by 9th Welch and proceeded to Brigade School in camp at N.15.a.	" " N. 15.a.
"	26th		Day spent on general cleaning up – inspections – and bathing.	" "
"	27		Working parties were found on the day totalling 2 Officers & 116 other ranks and at night 5 Officers & 215 men – under the R.E.	" "
"	28		A working party of 112 men and 2 Officers were found on the day and at night 5 Officers & 212 men for work under R.E. 3 men were wounded this night.	" "
"	29		Further working parties found – on the day 1 Officer and 118 men and at night 4 Officers & 217 men. 1 Man wounded in the evening.	" "
"	30		Working parties comprising 1 Officer and 115 men were found this day and at night 4 Officers & 175 Men. 1 Man wounded.	" "

August 1916. Sheet 2.

WAR DIARY
or
INTELLIGENCE SUMMARY

Army Form C. 2118

Place	Date	Hour	Summary of Events and Information	Remarks and references to Appendices
N.KEMMEL	Aug 1916			
	25		During the period Battalion was in Brigade Reserve leaving was not possible owing to large number of working parties that had to be found. Few men that were available were mostly employed in cleaning up and improving the Camps. Battalion relieved 9th Welch in the Trenches taking over same line as on 19th inst. "C" & "D" Company in the firing line. "A" in Support "B" Company in Reserve - Company of 75/77 Canadians were attached to "B" for instruction.	M. N. 18 c. N. 24 c. do. "

Walters Lt-Col

Comdg. 6th (S) Battn. Wiltshire Regt.

vol 15

Confidential

War diary

of

6 (S) Bn Wiltshire Regt.

from 1st to 30th Sept. 1916.

Volume 15.

WAR DIARY
or
INTELLIGENCE SUMMARY.
(Erase heading not required.)

Army Form C. 2118.

Instructions regarding War Diaries and Intelligence Summaries are contained in F.S. Regs., Part II and the Staff Manual respectively. Title pages will be prepared in manuscript.

Place	Date	Hour	Summary of Events and Information	Remarks and references to Appendices
KEMMEL	1916 Sept 1		Night of 31st Aug. Battalion relieved 9th Welch in trenches from H.1 to E.KIN. A & B Companies in the firing line. C in support. D in support. Coy "D" Canadians attached to each company for instruction. Relief carried out by 36 Battalion on 57 Brigade front with artillery cooperation. Slight bombardment by enemy on our front line. Casualties were 2 killed and 1 wounded. Remainder of day fairly quiet with very quiet night.	MESSINES N180 – N24C
"	" 2		Very quiet day. Work continued in improving trenches. One man wounded.	al N19a
"	" 3		Battalion relieved by 73 & 38 1st Canadians. Proceeded to bivouac at BUTTERFLY camp.	al
"	" 4		Battalion left BUTTERFLY camp at 4.15am and proceeded by stages at DE SEULE. Very wet day. Lt. Col. Langley joined from 19th Hussars.	
DE SEULE	" 5		Very wet day – Day spent in general cleaning up and arranging camp and ARMENTIERES B10	ARMENTIERES B10
"	" 6		Weather very much improved. Platoon training etc.	al
"	" 7		Platoon training. Open signal drill. Concert in the afternoon	al
"	" 8		Battalion relieved 1st Argyll Sutherland Highlanders on outpost at CHAPELLE ROMPUE – A & D Companies occupying posts and being moved up in support. B & C Welch in front at N7c line. Capt. Smith attended a French trench demonstration at ARMENTIERES in the afternoon.	N7c
CHAPELLE ROMPUE	" 9		Commanding Officer, Capt. Smith, Capt. Nairn, Capt. Fulton Practical Officers attended an Anti gas course in the morning. Civil squad out – Cleaning up billets etc these having been left in a dirty condition by the outgoing unit.	al
"	" 10		Sunday – Church Parade.	al

WAR DIARY
or
INTELLIGENCE SUMMARY.
(Erase heading not required.)

Army Form C. 2118.

Instructions regarding War Diaries and Intelligence Summaries are contained in F. S. Regs., Part II. and the Staff Manual respectively. Title pages will be prepared in manuscript.

Place	Date	Hour	Summary of Events and Information	Remarks and references to Appendices
	1916			ARMENTIERES.
CHAPELLE D'ARMENTIERES	Jan 11.		Battalion filled out with new 2nd Lieutenants – having same by passing through Gas Chamber under supervision of medical officer.	N/C
"	" 12.		Army signal duty – Our artillery active wire cutting.	" "
"	" 13.		Battalion relieved 9th Welch in trenches (right sector) from Trench 93 to Trench 98. "B" Company on right – "D" on centre – "A" on left – "C" in support. Relief took place in the afternoon. Wire cutting operations by our artillery continued on that of our front and that of Battalion on our left.	" "
"	" 14.		Wire cutting operations commenced at 11.30 a.m. Enemy field minenwerfer chiefly about Tip of Long Avenue and Essex Avenue.	" "
"	" 15.		Raid made by Battalion on Left Sector and by Brigade on right. Slight retaliation on our front by enemy minenwerfer rifle grenades.	" "
"	" 16.		Day spent in improving damaged barren wire broken – Enemy quiet.	" "
"	" 17.		2nd R. Wing reformed from England.	" "
"	" 18.		Wire in trenches continued. Our casualties were 4 wounded one of whom died the following day.	" "
"	" 19.		Battalion relieved by 9 Devons in the afternoon and proceeded to billets at NIEPPE.	" "
"	" 20.		Battalion moved to MEERIS arriving at about 3.30 p.m. Very wet day.	2.Y. HAZEBROUCK 5A.
"	" 21.		Day spent in general cleaning up.	" "
"	" 22. & 23.		Platoon Training – Class of instruction for NCO's under Regimental Sergeant Major Bates.	" "

WAR DIARY
or
INTELLIGENCE SUMMARY.

(Erase heading not required.)

Army Form C. 2118.

Place	Date	Hour	Summary of Events and Information	Remarks and references to Appendices
HAZEBROUCK	1916 Sept 24		Sunday.	at HAZEBROUCK S.H.
"	" 25		Coys. Squad Drill. Company training in the morning. Class of instruction for N.C.Os. under Regimental Sergt Major, in the afternoon. Battalion together with remainder of 158 Brigade were inspected by G.O.C. 2nd Army, Genl Plumer. Sgt Tanner injured.	"
"	" 26		Platoon training - Class for N.C.Os. as on previous day. Bathe - football in the afternoon.	"
"	" 27 28 & 29		Company Training - Class for N.C.Os. under Regimental Sergt Major.	"
"	" 30		Platoon training. Class for N.C.Os. under Regimental Sergt Major. - Battalion played the 9th Cheshire Regt. in the afternoon in the divisional football Competition. Kaver, C.Wells, 1, 9th Cheshire 3.	"

Walker
Lt-Col
Comdg 6/Bn Welch Regiment

vol 16

Confidential

War Diary

of

6th Bn Wiltshire Regt.

From 1st Oct. to 31st Oct. 1916.

Volume — 16.

WAR DIARY
or
INTELLIGENCE SUMMARY.
(Erase heading not required.)

Army Form C. 2118.

Place	Date	Hour	Summary of Events and Information	Remarks and references to Appendices
MERRIS	1 Oct		Sunday - Church Parade.	at LENS
"	2 "		Company Platoon Training - Bombing Instruction. Class of Instruction	SHEET 112
"	3 "		for N.C.O.s under Regimental Sergeant Major.	at "
"	4 "			"
"	5 "		Battalion left MERRIS at about 4pm and entrained at BAILLEUL STATION	"
"	6 "		at 10pm arriving at DOULLENS at about 6am on 6". From here bn	"
			proceeded to camp near AUTHIE.	
"	7 "		Battalion moved to ROSSIGNOL FARM, M¹ COUGNEUX in Brigade Reserve.	"
"	8 "		Sunday - Company inspections in fighting order.	at "
"	9 "		Usual Company inspections - Working parties found in morning	"
"	10 "		and afternoon. Battalion had baths.	"
"	11 "			"
"	12 "			"
"	13 "		Battalion relieved 9" Cheshires in trenches in HEBUTERNE SECTOR.	at HEBUTERNE
			"A" & "B" Companies in the firing line, "C" in support & "D" in reserve.	"
			Relief took place in the afternoon.	

WAR DIARY
or
INTELLIGENCE SUMMARY.

(Erase heading not required.)

Army Form C. 2118.

Instructions regarding War Diaries and Intelligence Summaries are contained in F. S. Regs., Part II. and the Staff Manual respectively. Title pages will be prepared in manuscript.

Place	Date	Hour	Summary of Events and Information	Remarks and references to Appendices
	Oct.			
IN THE TRENCHES	14.		Our artillery very active wire cutting. Enemy retaliation slight.	Pl. HEBUTERNE MAP SHEET
	15.		Usual work done by parties at night. 2nd Lt. Atkinson was wounded early in the morning of 14th. Major Goffey 9 Wilts Regt took over Command of Batt. on 14th during temporary absence of Lt-Col. Long. Our casualties during this period in trenches were 2 other ranks killed and 2 wounded.	" "
"	16		Battalion relieved in the afternoon by 12th Battn of 22nd Brigade and proceeded by bus to billets at VAUCHELLES.	MAP SHEET 57 d N.E.
VAUCHELLES	17		Battalion moved to billets at HERRISART.	" "
HERRISART	18		Day spent in general cleaning up – during which weather parade were not possible. On 20th Batt. left HERRISART and also marching some little way orders received that Battalion should return to HERRISART.	" "
	19.			
	20.			
	21		Very wet day – Company inspection Lectures	" "
	22.		Bonn left HERRISART and proceeded to billets in BOUZINCOURT. 2nd Bngg. Orders found from 143rd & 8th Hants not available for reference.	m 57 d SE
BOUZINCOURT	23		Battalion proceeded to dugouts at CRUCIFIX CORNER MEAVELY in relief	"

Army Form C. 2118.

WAR DIARY
or
INTELLIGENCE SUMMARY.
(Erase heading not required.)

Instructions regarding War Diaries and Intelligence Summaries are contained in F. S. Regs., Part II. and the Staff Manual respectively. Title pages will be prepared in manuscript.

Place	Date	Hour	Summary of Events and Information	Remarks and references to Appendices
CRUCIFX CORNER	24		of 3rd Worcester Regiment. Working party of 200 was found in the afternoon carrying ammunition.	57d S.E.
"	25		Company employed – Working parties were found in morning and afternoon & night carrying ammunition.	"
"	26		Battalion relieved 8th Gloucests Regiment in REGINA & STUFF trenches at	"
IN THE TRENCHES	16		B" Company on the left, D" in the centre, C" on the right – A" Company in STUFF REDOUBT.	"
"	30th		A" Company being in support. Headquarters in STUFF REDOUBT. Enemy artillery active say night – Chiefly on Regina front. Companys trenches and STUFF Redoubt. Our casualties were four killed and eighteen wounded. Battalion relieved by 8th Devonshire Regt. and proceeded to camp nr. CRUCIFIX CORNER.	"
"	31		Day spent in general cleaning up.	8.

2/10/16

Walt Long
[signature] Lt Col
Commanding 8th Worcester Regt.
11/62

Confidential

Vol 17.

War Diary

of

6th (S) Bn Wiltshire Regt

From 1/11/16 to 30/11/16

Volume 17.

WAR DIARY
or
INTELLIGENCE SUMMARY.
(Erase heading not required.)

Army Form C. 2118.

Instructions regarding War Diaries and Intelligence Summaries are contained in F. S. Regs., Part II. and the Staff Manual respectively. Title pages will be prepared in manuscript.

Place	Date	Hour	Summary of Events and Information	Remarks and references to Appendices
Nr AVELUY	Nov 1	-	Day spent in general cleaning up.	MAP SHEET 57d SE.
"	" 2	-	Battalion relieved 8th Gloucester Regt in STUFF & REGINA Trenches - B, C & D Companies in firing line and "A" in support. Headquarters on STUFF Redoubt.	W.18.a
IN THE TRENCHES	" 3 & 4	-	During relief enemy artillery were very active causing some 30 casualties. During this tour in trenches state of trenches very bad indeed.	R.21.
"	R 5		enemy artillery continuously shelling. On the 3rd 2nd Lt. J. Greene was killed. Our total casualties were 13 other ranks killed, 43 wounded and 1 Missing. On the night of 5/6 Battalion were relieved by 4th South Lancs Regt and proceeded to billets in AVELUY	at R.17.a
AVELUY	" 6th	-	Day spent in cleaning up	at R.17.a.
"	" 7th	-	Usual company inspections. Some of the men had baths.	"
"			2nd Draft of 120 ORs from 4th W.Yorks joined.	"
"	" 8th		Nearly all available men for work were employed unloading trains at AVELUY STATION from 6am to 10pm both these days.	"
"	" 9th			"
"	" 10		Usual company inspection - Working party of 30 men unloading	"

WAR DIARY
or
INTELLIGENCE SUMMARY.
(Erase heading not required.)

Army Form C. 2118.

Place	Date	Hour	Summary of Events and Information	Remarks and references to Appendices
AVELUY	Nov 11.		Batn at AVELUY STATION.	a.g Map Sheet 57d SE. R.21.
	" 12.		Battalion relieved 8 N. Staffs Regt in front line and "C" in support. A, B & D Companies in firing line and "C" in support.	ab
IN THE TRENCHES.	" 13.		Enemy very active with their artillery - Capt Smith was killed & 2nd Lt Beck wounded on 13th. Casualties, other ranks 0 killed & 12 wounded. Battn relieved on night of 14/15 by 9 Welch Regiment proceeded to dugouts in old German line near AUTHILLE WOOD.	"
Nr AUTHILLE WOOD	" 14			ab
IN THE TRENCHES	" 15		Battalion relieved 7th & Lancs in front line - A. B & C Companies in firing line and "D" in reserve. Capt Tanner & 2nd Lt.	"
	" 16.		Cowan were wounded on 16th. On 16th "A" Company were relieved by a Company of 9th Royal Welsh Fusiliers and went into reserve on left of "D" Company. Casualties were 9 other ranks wounded.	"
	" 17		Battalion relieved by 10 Warwicks proceeded to huts at CRUCIFIX CORNER. 2nd Lt Baylis from R.A.M.C. joined.	ag N18a
Nr AVELUY	" 18		Day spent in general cleaning up.	"

Army Form C. 2118.

WAR DIARY
or
INTELLIGENCE SUMMARY.
(Erase heading not required.)

Instructions regarding War Diaries and Intelligence Summaries are contained in F. S. Regs., Part II. and the Staff Manual respectively. Title pages will be prepared in manuscript.

Place	Date	Hour	Summary of Events and Information	Remarks and references to Appendices
Mt AVELUY	Nov 19		Battalion relieved Battalions of 5th Brigade (after their attack) in front line. STUFF TRENCH. Headquarters in Hessian Trench.	MAP SHEET 57^d SE.
"	"20		Enemy inactive on LUCKY WAY - Lieut Brown did invaluable work on patrol on daytime on many occasions. German line - 061 and found line unoccupied. Two trench mortar aparatus occupied by "C" Company and consolidated. Our casualties were 14 other ranks wounded. H	R 21
IN THE TRENCHES.	"21			
"			Killed 1 Missing. Lt Col Long took over command of 56th Brigade on 20th. Major Carlyon took over Command of the Battalion	"
"	"22		Battalion relieved by 13th Northumberland Fusiliers of 61st Division and proceeded to huts at CRUCIFIX CORNER.	W 18 a
Mt AVELUY	"23		Battalion moved to WARLOY.	LENS SHEET
WARLOY	"24		Battalion left WARLOY and proceeded to DOULLENS staying there for 1 night.	11 A
DOULLENS	"25		Battalion continued its march and proceeded to BOISBERGUES.	"
BOISBERGUES	"26		Very wet day. A draft of 70 other ranks arrived.	"
	"27 "28		Day spent in general cleaning up drying clothes. Company inspection + arm drill.	"

Army Form C. 2118.

WAR DIARY
or
INTELLIGENCE SUMMARY.
(Erase heading not required.)

Instructions regarding War Diaries and Intelligence Summaries are contained in F. S. Regs., Part II. and the Staff Manual respectively. Title pages will be prepared in manuscript.

Place	Date	Hour	Summary of Events and Information	Remarks and references to Appendices
BOISBERGUES	29		Usual Company inspections - baths.	at LENS
	30		G.O.C. 58 Infantry Brigade inspected the new draft.	2J SHEET 11.
	30/11/1916		A Carlyon Major	
			Comnd'g 6 Bn Wiltshire Regiment.	

Vol 18

Confidential

War Diary
— of —

6th (S) Bn Wiltshire Regiment.

From 1st to 31st December 1916

Volume 18.

Army Form C. 2118.

WAR DIARY
or
INTELLIGENCE SUMMARY.
(Erase heading not required.)

Instructions regarding War Diaries and Intelligence Summaries are contained in F. S. Regs., Part II. and the Staff Manual respectively. Title pages will be prepared in manuscript.

Place	Date	Hour	Summary of Events and Information	Remarks and references to Appendices
BOISBERGUES	1916 Dec 1.		Platoon training – Arm drill – a draft of 60 other ranks arrived.	This LENS SHEET
"	2.		Company drill – Football in the afternoon.	" 11.
"	3.		Sunday – Church parade.	"
"	4.		Company drill – Bombing instruction under the Battalion Bombing Officer – Class of instruction for N.C.O's under the Regimental Sergeant Major.	"
"	5.		Company training – Bombing – Boxing in the afternoon – Draft of 51 other ranks arrived.	"
"	6.		Platoon training – Class of instruction for N.C.O's under the Regimental Sergeant Major. On the 8th G.O.C. 58 Infantry Brigade inspected the new drafts. L-Col. Lord O.S. Thynne joined Battalion on the 8th. Battalion Cross Country run held on afternoon of 9th.	"
"	7. }			7.11
"	8. }			"
"	9. }		Draft of 11 other ranks joined on 9th.	7.11
"	10.		Sunday – Church Parade.	"
"	11. }		Platoon training – Bombing – Lewis Gun Class – Lewis Gun Class of Instruction for N.C.O's under the Regimental Sergeant Major. Recreation in the afternoon.	"
"	12. }			"
"	13.		G.O.C. 58 Corps inspected the Battalion on the morning – Brigade Cross Country Run in the afternoon.	"
"	14. }		Platoon training – Sports in the afternoon. Bombing instruction – Wiring – Musketry. On 15th the Battalion played the 2nd Cheshire Regt on 14th.	"
"	15. }			"
"	16.		No Brigade Competition owing 2 – 1.	"
"	17.		Sunday – Church Parade. A draft of 104 other ranks (infantry) arrived.	"
"	18. }		Company training – Lewis Class of Instruction for N.C.O's under Regimental Sergeant Major – Musketry – Bombing – Lewis Gun Class – Bayonet fighting – Recreation Training in the afternoon – Divisional Tour were held at BERMAINE on afternoon of 21st.	"
"	19. }			"
"	20. }			"
"	21. }		2nd Lt. R.W. Barton wounded previously on 22nd. New draft of midshipmen continued it.	"
"	22. }			"
"	23. }		Training carried out at MORLOW	"

Army Form C. 2118.

WAR DIARY
or
INTELLIGENCE SUMMARY.
(Erase heading not required.)

Instructions regarding War Diaries and Intelligence Summaries are contained in F. S. Regs., Part II. and the Staff Manual respectively. Title pages will be prepared in manuscript.

Place	Date	Hour	Summary of Events and Information	Remarks and references to Appendices
BOIS BERGUES	Dec 26		Sunday – Church Parade.	R/LENS SHEET
"	" 26		Christmas Day.	11.
	" 26		A working party of 50 Men found daily from 26th to 31st for work at FEINVILLERS under O.C. 148th R.E. Company R.E. Another working party of 150 Men were employed daily introducing in BOIS FLEURI from 26th to 31st. Remainder of Battalion continued Platoon training – Bombing Lewis Gun Classes – Instruction for NCOs under the Regimental Sergt Major – Wiring instruction – Musketry – A draft of 3 Officers and arrived on 27th, 1 C.P. Bono from No.1 Signal Company R.E. joined Us Battalion for duty on 29th.	

20/1/6/

R.G. Taylor Lt Col.
Commanding 6 Br Victoria Regt

Vol 19

Confidential

War diary
of
6th (S) 82nd Wiltshire Regiment
From 1st to 31st January 1945

Volume 19

WAR DIARY or INTELLIGENCE SUMMARY

Army Form C. 2118.

Place	Date 1917 Jany	Hour	Summary of Events and Information	Remarks and references to Appendices
BOISBERGUES	1 to 6	—	Platoon & Company training. Classes of Instruction for NCO's under Regimental Sergt. Major. Bombing & Lewis Gun Classes. Bayonet fighting & Physical training. Musketry.	LENS SHEET 11
"	7	"	Sunday - Church Parade.	"
"	8	"	Arm drill. Kit Inspection etc.	"
"	9	"	Battalion left BOISBERGUES proceeding to billets at BEAUVAL.	"
BEAUVAL	10	"	Batt.n & Lewis gun section. 2/ Savage from Details joined.	"
"	11	"	Day spent on general cleaning up - Arms drill etc.	"
"	12	"	Battalion made an early start moving by Motor Lorry to SAILLY. Relieved the 13 Yorks Lanc. Regt in HEBUTERNE Sector - "A" & "C" Coys 9th R.W.Fusiliers attached 16.73½. The first named Company being the left front Company, the Coker, left support Company. "D" Company 6th Wilts going into the centre front line, "B" Company, Centre support, 2nd Coy on right front and "A" Coy right support.	57d N.E.
HEBUTERNE	13	—	Inter Company relief - "D" Company 9.R.W.Fusiliers relieving "A" Company 9 R.H.Fusilirs. "B" Company 6 Wilts relieving "D" Company 6 Wilts. "A" Coy 6 Wilts relieving "C" Company. 1 man killed & 1 wounded.	"
"	14	—	Enemy artillery active shelling HEBUTERNE. 1 man killed by evening.	"
"	15	—	"B" & "D" Companies 6 Wilts relieved by 2 Companies 9 R.H.Fusiliers & 6 Wilts in Reserve at SAILLY. 2/Lt. Holdell from B/Wilts etc.	"

WAR DIARY
or
INTELLIGENCE SUMMARY.
(Erase heading not required.)

Army Form C. 2118.

Place	Date Jany 1917	Hour	Summary of Events and Information	Remarks and references to Appendices
SAILLY	16		2nd Lieut. A. Bailey and 3rd O.R.s joined for duty.	see Appx. "A"
			Working parties found in morning returning by 8.30. 3 Companies - D Company detailed as support Company to Battalion in the Line. Lt. Granger Arrived.	
"	17 18		Work & rests found for duty. Working parties found by B & D Companies both these days.	"
"	19		"A" & "C" Companies relieved from the Line by 2 Companies 9th R.W. Fusiliers & moved to Huts in the DELL Nr SAILLY.	"
"	20		Working parties found by A, C & D Companies.	"
"	21 22		Working Parties found both these days — Enemy artillery active shelling SAILLY on 21st. 3 men killed & 4 wounded when returning from working party.	"
"	23		Battalion relieved 9th Welch Regiment in trenches in HEBUTERNE SECTOR. "A" Coy in right front line, "D" in left front line, "C" Coy night support. "B" left support. 2nd Lt. Williams & Lt. Matthews admitted to Hospital Sick.	"
HEBUTERNE	24		Enemy Trench communicating trenches and support line heavily shelled.	"
	25		Inter Company relief between B & D Companies. 2/5 West Riding Regt attacked to Battalion for instruction. Enemy Artillery active on advanced post 5.30 pm to 6.30 pm.	"

WAR DIARY
or
INTELLIGENCE SUMMARY.

Army Form C. 2118.

(Erase heading not required.)

Place	Date 1917 Jany	Hour	Summary of Events and Information	Remarks and references to Appendices
HEBUTERNE	26		"D" Company relieved "B" in front line. Enemy artillery active.	ref 57 N.E.
"	27		Battalion relieved by 9 Welch Regt. B, D Companies + H.Q. proceeding to huts in the DELL and A + C Companies to SAILLY. "A" Company etc were detailed as supports to Battalion on the line	
SAILLY	28		Day spent in general cleaning up — Working parties found. Rev. received that Brigadier General Long was killed in action this day	sd "
"	29		Working parties found. Funeral of Brig. Genl Long took place at Couin Cemetery this Battalion finding a Firing Party.	sd "
"	30		Working parties found.	
"	31		Battalion relieved 9 Welch in HEBUTERNE Sector. "C" Company right front line. "D" Coy Left front. "B" right support. "A" Coy left support. 2 Platoons of 18 West Yorks Regt attached to Battalion. On relief 2 Plats of 6 Welch inadvertently returned to our Reserve at 78 West York. 4 Casualties	"

3/2/1917.

A.J. Thynne
Lt Col
Comm'g 6/18 Wiltshire Regt

Vol 20

Confidential

War Diary

— of —

6" (S) B" Wiltshire Regiment.

From 1st to 28th February 1917.

Volume 20.

Army Form C. 2118.

WAR DIARY
or
INTELLIGENCE SUMMARY.
(Erase heading not required.)

Instructions regarding War Diaries and Intelligence Summaries are contained in F. S. Regs. Part II. and the Staff Manual respectively. Title pages will be prepared in manuscript.

Place	Date	Hour	Summary of Events and Information	Remarks and references to Appendices
In the Trenches HEBUTERNE	Feby 1st		Enemy artillery active firing a few shells into JENA Trenches - Advanced Posts relieved every 12 hours.	MAP SHEET 57d NE
	2nd		"A" Company relieved "D" Company in firing line and "B" Company relieved "C" HEBUTERNE shelled slightly in afternoon. Working Parties found for R.E.	"
"	3.		Enemy active with artillery in the early morning - Working Parties for R.E.	"
"	4.		Battalion relieved by 9th Welch and proceeded to billets in Reserve. A B & C Companies into the Bell and "D" Company to SAILLY the Company being detailed as support Company to the Battalion in the Line	"
SAILLY	5.		Day spent in general cleaning up, resting baths.	"
"	6.		10 Platoons found for work. Remainder of Battalion doing Platoon training.	"
"	7.		10½ Platoons found for work - Remainder of Battalion carrying on Platoon training. 2nd Lt. Friend. Badgley Rankin Rooks 3rd Wells joined for duty - A draft of 90 other ranks arrived.	"

FEBRUARY 1917. SHEET 1.

WAR DIARY
or
INTELLIGENCE SUMMARY.
(Erase heading not required.)

Army Form C. 2118.

Place	Date	Hour	Summary of Events and Information	Remarks and references to Appendices
SAILLY	Feby 8.		Working parties found - Platoon drill - In the evening Battalion turned out in response to an S.O.S. signal from the front line - "D" Company proceeding to the Battalion in the front line - It was found that the signal was not sent up by anyone on our front extension "D" Coy returned to billets in SAILLY.	MAP SHEET 57 N.E.
"	9.		Working parties found - Arm & grade drill - Lecture by Major BROCKLEHURST of 3rd Somerset Light Infantry given in the evening	d[itt]o
"	10.		Working parties - Platoon training - Kit Inspections.	d[itt]o
"	11.		Company training - draft of 23 other ranks arrived - Lecture by Major BROCKLEHURST to all N.C.Os. on the War Loan.	d[itt]o
"	12.		Company training - Lecture by Capt TYNAN on Scouting & Patrol work.	d[itt]o
"	13.		Demonstration by Special Platoon of "A" Coy in the morning which all N.C.Os attended - Remainder of Battalion went for a route march under the Adjutant. A bayonet fighting class for all N.C.Os under C.S.M. HEWITT. in the afternoon	d[itt]o
"	14.		Platoon & Company training - N.C.Os. under C.S.M. HEWITT. for bayonet fighting instruction on the afternoon	d[itt]o

February 1917 - SHEET 2.

WAR DIARY or INTELLIGENCE SUMMARY

Army Form C. 2118.

Place	Date 1917	Hour	Summary of Events and Information	Remarks and references to Appendices
SAILLY	Feby 15 & 16		Battalion Training – Practice attack carried out under C.O's. HENITTIN on on previous days. On 16th Regimental Concert in the evening – Lt. Stevens & 2nd Lt. Atkinson from 3rd Wilts joined together with a draft of 26 other ranks. 2nd Lt's Skeggo & Kent from Cadet School joined also.	MAPSHEET 57d NE
"	17.		Battalion relieved 8th North Staffordshire Regt. of 51st Brigade on L1 Sector – D. Company being the left front company, C. Company right front, A. Company left support and B. Company right support – Headquarters in GETORIX Trench.	"
"	18.		Supplied working parties for R.E., carrying duckboards from EUSTON to NAIRN Trench. Enemy fairly quiet.	"
"	19.		Intn. Company relief – A. Company relieving D. & B. Company relieving C.	"
"	20.		Battalion relieved by 12th East Yorks. of 9th Division and proceeded to billets in LOUVENCOURT. During this period in trenches enemy Artillery shelled our front lines slightly – 2 our casualties were 3 other ranks wounded.	"
LOUVENCOURT	21.		Resting – General cleaning up.	MAPSHEET 57d LENS 11.

WAR DIARY
or
INTELLIGENCE SUMMARY.
(Erase heading not required.)

Army Form C. 2118.

Place	Date	Hour	Summary of Events and Information	Remarks and references to Appendices
LOUVEN COURT	22 1917		Two Companies working digging trenches for training. Remainder of Battalion carrying on Platoon training. 2nd Lt. Lenks from 9th Wilts joined on 23rd.	MAP SHEET 57d LENS II.
	23			
	24			
	25			
"	26		Battalion Training - Battalion carrying out an attack practice. 2nd Lt Finlay from Cadet School joined - A draft of 5 other ranks joined.	"
"	27.		Brigade Training - Attack formation	
"	28.		Platoon Training - Arms drill etc. 58th Brigade relieved 57 Brigade in Trenches, 9 Wilts relieving a Battalion of 57 Brigade in newly captured trenches between SERRE & RISIEUX.	

1/2/1917.

A.G. Thynne Lt-Col
Comdg 6th (S) Battn. Wiltshire Regt.

Confidential   No 21

War Diary
—of—
6th Bn. Wiltshire Regt.

From 1st to 31st March 1917.

Volume 21

Army Form C. 2118.

WAR DIARY
or
INTELLIGENCE SUMMARY.
(Erase heading not required.)

Instructions regarding War Diaries and Intelligence Summaries are contained in F. S. Regs. Part II. and the Staff Manual respectively. Title pages will be prepared in manuscript.

Place	Date 1917	Hour	Summary of Events and Information	Remarks and references to Appendices
LOUVENCOURT	Mch 1.		Battalion marched from LOUVENCOURT to Camp at EUSTON POST. Camps slightly shelled during the afternoon. 1 Man was killed.	LENS SHEET 11.
EUSTON CAMP.	" 2.		Relieved 9th Bn Welch Regiment in St DAVID and ROSSIGNOL Trenches in PUISIEUX - A.D.G. B Companies in front line and "C" Company in reserve. Engaged post on right held by enemy and established line of posts in advance of French and got into communication with 2nd Division on right and also on left about ROSSIGNOL WOOD.	LENS SHEET 11.
PUISIEUX	" 3.		Daylight patrol up KNIFE & FORK trench to FORK WOOD gaining touch with enemy. Patrol returned. Artillery put on position held by enemy who were later observed to be following Northward towards BUCQUOY. Our casualties were 3 other ranks wounded. Battalion relieved by 11th East Yorks of 31st Division and proceeded to EUSTON CAMP.	
EUSTON CAMP.	" 4.		Battalion moved to billets at YEW CAMP Nr BUS.	
YEW CAMP BUS.	" 5.		Day spent in general cleaning up - Baths - Resting.	
"	" 6.		One Company found for work - Remainder of Battalion route marching. The Commanding Officer proceeded on 10 days leave (UK)	
"	" 7.			
"	" 8.		Battalion route march both these days.	
"	" 9.			
"	" 10.		Battalion started on its march to the North staying at BEAUVAL the night.	

WAR DIARY
or
INTELLIGENCE SUMMARY.

(Erase heading not required.)

Army Form C. 2118.

Place	Date 1917	Hour	Summary of Events and Information	Remarks and references to Appendices
BEAUVAL	Mch 11	—	Battalion continued the march arriving at NEUVILLETTE in the BOURDENAISON area.	LENS SHEET 11.
NEUVILLETTE	" 12	—	General cleaning up etc. Arms drill.	A.A.
"	" 13	—	Battalion marched to NUNCQ on the FLERS area.	A.A.
NUNCQ	" 14	—	Battalion proceeded to billets at BOURS in the PERNES area.	A.A.
BOURS	" 15	—	Resting.	A.A.
"	" 16	—	Moved to AUCHY-AU-BOIS in the ST HILAIRE area.	A.A. LENS SHEET 11 & HAZEBROUCK 5A.
AUCHY-AU-BOIS	" 17	—	Resting and recreation.	A.A. HAZEBROUCK 5A.
"	" 18	—	Battalion moved to BOISENGHEM. Commanding Officer returned from leave.	A.A.
BOISENGHEM	" 19	—	Marched to STRAZEELE in MEREIS area.	"
STRAZEELE	" 20	—	Moved to billets in ROUGE CROIX. N° CAISTRE.	"
ROUGE CROIX	" 21	—	Company training - Class of Instruction for N.C.O.s under 2nd Lt. G. Richard.	"
"	" 22	—	20 N.C.Os detailed for work on Farm at FLETRE, Platoon training. N.C.O.s under 2nd Lt. G. Richard.	"

WAR DIARY
or
INTELLIGENCE SUMMARY.

Army Form C. 2118.

(Erase heading not required.)

Place	Date	Hour	Summary of Events and Information	Remarks and references to Appendices
ROCE CROIX	23ʳᵈ 23,24	-	Commanding Officer proceeded to 2n Army Schools on Battalion Commanders tour.	
"	25	-	Company + Platoon training. Class of N.C.Os. under King 2nd Lt. L. Pritchard. Kindia - Testing 2nd Ot. from 3rd W.R.a. joined together with a draft of 21 other ranks	M/ HAZEBROUCK 5A.
"	26	-	on 25th and 11 O.Rs. and 25 Other Ranks proceeded to BAILLEU for attending courses. Inspection of Battalion by G.O.C. by Army Commander. 2nd Lt. Badgley together with flet	
"	27	-	other ranks proceeded to STEENBECQUE to attend course.	"
"	28	-	Company + Platoon training - Class of NCOs under 2nd Lt L Pritchard.	
"	29	-	G.O.C. 5th Brigade inspected the Regimental Transport on 28ᵗʰ —	
"	30.	-	2nd Lt Begg from 3rd W.R.a joined on 27ᵗʰ.	
"	31.	-	Battalion relieved 10th Warwicks in reserve at RIDGE WOOD in DICKEBUSCH Sector.	Ap. 28 "S.W."
			Commanding Officer returned from tour.	

Alf Myers Lt-Col
Commanding Wiltshire Regt

Vol 22

Confidential

War Diary
— of —
6(S). Bn Wiltshire Regiment.

From 1st April to 30th April 191..

Volume 22.

WAR DIARY
or
INTELLIGENCE SUMMARY.
(Erase heading not required.)

Army Form C. 2118.

Place	Date 1917	Hour	Summary of Events and Information	Remarks and references to Appendices
RIDGE WOOD	April 1st	—	Working party of 1 Officer 150 other ranks found for work on gaps in front line between POPPY LANE & CHICORY TRENCH (N.12.2.23. – O.7.a.33). A draft of 51 other ranks arrived.	WYTSCHAETE 28 S.W. 1/10000 (N.5a).
"	2nd	—	Enemy artillery active shelling N.W. edge of RIDGE WOOD (N.5.a.7.) between 10 and 11 am. also at 10 pm. One man was wounded. Working party found for work on gaps in front line as yesterday.	"
"	3rd	—	Enemy shelled RIDGE WOOD slightly at 5am and 4pm.	"
"	4th	—	Battalion relieved 9 Royal Welsh Fusiliers in left subsector of DIEPENDAAL Sector. 2 Platoons of "B" Company in front line from O.7.c.19. – O.7.a.95. and 2 Platoons in New Redan Line from N.18.b.98. to O.1.c.3.1. "C" Company in front line from O.7.b.25 to O.7.b.6.95. "A" Company in Redoubts as follows:- WESTERN Redoubt O.1.c.2.0. N.12.a.80.95. – SOUTHERN Redoubt N.12.b.35. EASTERN Redoubt O.1.c.2.0. S.P.7. Redoubt O.1.c.2.0. D. Company in Reserve as follows:- 1 Platoon at N.12.a.95.95. 1 Platoon at N.12.a.9.9. 1 Platoon N.12.a.95.98 and the other Platoon from N.12.a.95.98 to N.12.b.4.7.	"
IN THE TRENCHES (DIEPENDAAL SECTOR).			Enemy artillery at intervals shelled RIDGE WOOD and area at N.5.a.8.8 between hours of 9.30 and 11am. Our artillery were cutting wire 18 pounders relation assisting. Enemy retaliated strongly with minenwerfers and rifle grenades. T.M. Bombs sent over by enemy several times during night and day. Our casualties were 9 wounded and 2	"

Army Form C. 2118.

WAR DIARY
or
INTELLIGENCE SUMMARY.
(Erase heading not required.)

Instructions regarding War Diaries and Intelligence Summaries are contained in F.S. Regs., Part II. and the Staff Manual respectively. Title pages will be prepared in manuscript.

Place	Date 1917	Hour	Summary of Events and Information	Remarks and references to Appendices
IN THE TRENCHES	5 Apl.	-	killed. Night of 4/5 Apl. a patrol of 1 Officer & 10 men left our lines at 0.7.a.3.2 their orders to Examine Enemy's wire entanglements to get close to enemy lines. Our artillery active - wire cutting - Enemy shelled our front line by way of retaliation - "C" Company endeavouring to raid Enemy line at new Reserve line. Our Lewis Gunners fired on enemy front line at about 2.30 pm, enemy retaliating with considerable force. A raid on our left by 16th Division at night was successful capturing 50 prisoners. A draft of 27 other ranks arrived. T.M.N. forces from Brasserie pond.	WYSCHAETE 28 S.W. [R]
"		6 am	Our artillery continued wire cutting operations - Enemy fired 2 or 3. 5.9's on P.O. Trench (O.1.2.) and also shelled S.E. edge of BOIS CARRÉ. The BRASSERIE at N.6.a.2.B was shelled heavily in afternoon. Our Stokes Mortars fired on enemy front line - enemy retaliating with T.M. bombs & trench mortar.	" [R]
"	7 "		Enemy shelled Chicory Trench with heavy shrapnel and whizzbangs between 4 & 5 pm. Area around the BRASSERIE shelled slightly about 2.30 pm. BRASSERIE was hit several times - RIDGE WOOD was also shelled very heavily between 3 pm & 3.15 pm. One man was wounded. The 41st Division on our left carried out a raid on German Front Line	" [R]

A5834 Wt. W4973 M687 750,000 8/16 D.D. & L. Ltd. Forms/C2118/13.

WAR DIARY
or
INTELLIGENCE SUMMARY.

Army Form C. 2118.

Place	Date 1917	Hour	Summary of Events and Information	Remarks and references to Appendices
IN THE TRENCHES	7 Oct. (contd)		system. Our front line was shelled – 2 Men being killed and 2 wounded.	AP
	8 "		Battalion relieved by 9" Cheshire Regiment and proceeded to DE ZON Camp (M.12.c.4.2).	FRANCE & BELGIUM 1/2 28.S.W.
DE ZON CAMP.	9 "		Company training – Battalion had baths	"
	10, 11, 12, 13, 14, 15.		"B" & "C" Companies of "D" Company practising daily an attack on entrenched raid on German front line – Remainder of Battalion Reserve Company training. On 14" L.O.C. 19" Division inspected DE ZON Camp. On evening of 15" Orders received that the anticipated raid on German line was cancelled.	AP " AP "
"	16 "		Battalion relieved 9" Welch Regiment in right subsector (DIXPENDAAL WYTSCHAETE Sector) from N.18.a.7.7. to O.7.c.1.9. "A" & "B" Companies in firing line. "D" & "C" Companies in support. Preparatory reconnaissance of route to German trenches at NAGS NOSE by Patrol.	1/2 28.S.N.
IN THE TRENCHES	17 "		A Patrol under 2 Officers of "C" Company made a reconnaissance of enemy trenches at NAGS NOSE. Enemy support line reached without opposition – trenches found to be in bad state and in some cases waterlogged. On reaching support line disarm were seen approaching in 3 parties of about 10 men each on either	AP

WAR DIARY
or
INTELLIGENCE SUMMARY.
(Erase heading not required.)

Army Form C. 2118.

Instructions regarding War Diaries and Intelligence Summaries are contained in F. S. Regs., Part II. and the Staff Manual respectively. Title pages will be prepared in manuscript.

Place	Date	Hour	Summary of Events and Information	Remarks and references to Appendices
IN THE TRENCHES.	18.		Plant Lcombe – Patrol then withdrew. Enemy artillery very quiet during two 2 days in trenches. Battalion relieved by 1st Royal Nova Scotia Regt of 56 Brigade and proceeded to CARNARVON CAMP. (M. 10 & 9.2)	FRANCE & BELGIUM 28. S.W. HAZEBROUCK 5A T.R.
CARNARVON CAMP	19		Battalion proceeded to billets at MONT des CATS near BOESCHEPPE.	T.R.
MONT des CATS.	20.) 21.)		Company training – Class of all N.C.O.s under 2nd Lt. A. Pritchard – Lewis Gun & Bombing instruction – Rifle grenade instruction –	T.R.
"	22.		Sunday. Church Parade.	"
"	23.		Company training – Class of N.C.O.s under 2nd Lt. A. Pritchard – Lewis Gun & Bombing instruction – Rifle grenade instruction. G.O.C. 19th Division inspected Battalion during training this day.	T.R.
"	24.) 25.)		Battalion carried out an attack practice. "Rifle grenadiers" given instruction under Divisional Bombing Officer.	T.R.
"	26.		Brigade training – attack practice in which aeroplanes took part.	T.R.
"	27.		Company Platoon training – Bombing instruction – Class for N.C.O.s under 2nd Lt. A. Pritchard.	T.R.

WAR DIARY
or
INTELLIGENCE SUMMARY.
(Erase heading not required.)

Army Form C. 2118.

Place	Date	Hour	Summary of Events and Information	Remarks and references to Appendices
MONT des CATS	27 (cont)		Commanding Officer inspected C + "D" Companies.	R/ HAZEB ROUG /R 5A.
"	28.		Company & Platoon training - Manual Lewis Guns & Bombing Classes. Commanding Officer inspected "A" + "B" Companies.	R/ FRANCE & BELGIUM SHEET 28.
"	29.		Battalion moved to SCOTTISH Camp at N G.23.a.75 relieving 10th Royal Irish Regiment of 68th Brigade.	R/
SCOTTISH CAMP.	30.		Battalion moved to YPRES in Brigade Reserve	R/ "

1/6/17.

Alu. Thynne
Lt Col
Commanding Leicestershire Regiment.

Confidential

Vol 23

6th Bn Wiltshire Regt.

War Diary

Volume 23

May 1917.

Army Form C. 2118.

WAR DIARY
or
INTELLIGENCE SUMMARY.
(Erase heading not required.)

Instructions regarding War Diaries and Intelligence Summaries are contained in F. S. Regs., Part II. and the Staff Manual respectively. Title pages will be prepared in manuscript.

Place	Date	Hour	Summary of Events and Information	Remarks and references to Appendices
YPRES.	1.5.17		Enemy shelled YPRES at intervals during the day. No casualties.	SHEET 28-S-W.
"	2.6.17		Ypres shelled slightly. 2nd Lt Coley and 3 OR wounded.	"
"	3.5.17		Enemy artillery very active all day. The Barracks receiving most attention. Being shelled very heavily about 11 am with 5.9's, 0.5.m pokes was killed and a S.M. Woodcock wounded. Our total casualties numbered 6 OR killed and 42 wounded.	"
"	4.5.17		Barracks again shelled at intervals during the morning. Battalion relieved 9th Cheshire Regt in the line A B and C D boys in front line. D boy in Support. Headquarters in ZILLEBEKE.	"
ZILLEBEKE	4/5		Our artillery fired on enemy's track areas and occasionally on enemy front line. Enemy at intervals fired whizzbangs into MAPLE COPSE. Otherwise quiet. Enemy airplane shot down by one of own airman just south of ZILLEBEKE.	ZILLEBEKE CH.
"	5/6		Our artillery fired 8 bdes on Railway line in vicinity of STIRLING CASTLE. Enemy shelled MAPLE COPSE and ZILLEBEKE with whizzbangs. Patrol sent out to examine enemy wire but owing to the brightness of the moon were unable to get close to enemy wire. 1 OR wounded.	"
"	6/7		Our artillery fired on enemy trenches in J.19.a and J.19.c about 9 pm. What appeared to be a small Grenade Dump exploded in vicinity of J.19.a 5.5. Four howitzer shells from our own batteries fell in vicinity of our front line between 6.30 and 9 pm. ZILLEBEKE was shelled during the night.	"

Army Form C. 2118.

WAR DIARY
or
INTELLIGENCE SUMMARY.
(Erase heading not required.)

Instructions regarding War Diaries and Intelligence Summaries are contained in F. S. Regs., Part II. and the Staff Manual respectively. Title pages will be prepared in manuscript.

Place	Date	Hour	Summary of Events and Information	Remarks and references to Appendices
ZILLEBEKE.	7/8th		Enemy shelled junction of front line and Sh Pit's Wood intermittently all day with whizzbangs. MENIN Road was also shelled from direction of STIRLING CASTLE. A hurricane bombardment from 8:45 to 9:00 pm was carried out by our artillery with the object of stopping the enemy shelling our back area at night. Enemy retaliated for about 5 minutes with shells of all calibres. The bombardment was repeated by us at 11:10 pm no retaliation followed.	ZILLEBEKE. (SHEET)
"	8/9th		Artillery quiet on both sides. Enemy trench mortars active on right front bay. Headquarters moved to DORMY HOUSE. 2 OR Wounded.	"
"	9/10th		At 7.80 pm enemy artillery commenced a general bombardment of our line and continued for half an hour. Several whizzbangs fell in vicinity of LOVERS WALK and Island WARRINGTON AVENUE. At 9.30 pm in response to S O S signals sent up on our right line our artillery put up a barrage on enemy front line. Enemy's aircraft active during the day. Enemy fired a few whizzbangs in vicinity of CRAB CRAWL WINNIPEG ST., LOVERS WALK and our front line were also shelled with 4.2's. Our artillery retaliated on enemy's front line and STIRLING CASTLE.	"
"	10/11th		Enemy artillery active shelling our back area throughout the day. Our front line also being whizzbanged at intervals. Enemy trench mortars also active on our front. Our artillery a.h.	"
"	11/12th			"

A 834 Wt W4975/M687 750,000 8/16 D. D. & L. Ltd. Forms/C.2118/13

Army Form C. 2118.

WAR DIARY
or
INTELLIGENCE SUMMARY.
(Erase heading not required.)

Instructions regarding War Diaries and Intelligence Summaries are contained in F.S. Regs., Part II. and the Staff Manual respectively. Title pages will be prepared in manuscript.

Place	Date	Hour	Summary of Events and Information	Remarks and references to Appendices
ZILLEBEKE	12/13th		On STIRLING CASTLE in the morning, and on enemy support line from St 40 - 6 pm.	SHEET. 28 S.W.
			Battalion relieved by the 8th ROYAL and proceeded to VANCOUVER CAMP. During this tour in trenches, the line was greatly improved. Dying his tour in trenches, the line was greatly improved and wire put along whole of Bath Front	A.Q
VANCOUVER CAMP.	18th		Battalion marched to MONT DES CATS	R.H. HAZEBROUCK 5.A.
MONT DES CATS	14th		Resting	A.Q.
"	15th		Battalion marched to WALLON CAPPELL staying there the night	A.Q
WALLON CAPPEL	16th		Battalion continued its march and proceeded to LINGHENESSE.	A.Q
LINGUENESSE	17th		Battalion proceeded to NORDASQUES. The Right Capt Blackwaite proceeded on Adv Guard at 2nd Army School WISQUES + CASSEL	A.Q.
NORDASQUES.	18th		Platoon & Company Training firing on miniature range.	A.Q.
"	19th		2 Companies on Range in morning - 2 in the afternoon	A.Q.
"	20th		Battalion scheme - attack practise. Draft of 25 joined Battalion.	A.Q.
"	21st		Brigade Training under Company arrangements.	A.Q.
"	22nd		Brigade Training under Company arrangements	A.Q
"	23rd		Brigade Training Brigade on the attack.	A.Q.
"	24th		Training under Bay arrangement. Transport marched to LONGUENESSE. Transport continued its march, proceeding to WALLON CAPPELL.	A.Q.
"	25th		Battalion moved to CURRAGH CAMP near LOCRE, proceeding by train from WATTEN to BAILLEUL. Transport continued its march marching to CURRAGH CAMP.	A.Q
CURRAGH CAMP	26th		Battalion inspected by G.O.C 19th Division, in Battle Order. Moved to	A.Q

WAR DIARY
or
INTELLIGENCE SUMMARY.
(Erase heading not required.)

Army Form C. 2118.

Instructions regarding War Diaries and Intelligence Summaries are contained in F. S. Regs., Part II. and the Staff Manual respectively. Title pages will be prepared in manuscript.

Place	Date	Hour	Summary of Events and Information	Remarks and references to Appendices
WESTON CAMP	27th		WESTON CAMP in the evening. Church Parade. Working Parties numbering .565 found in the evening. Adjutant reported from Bourse.	SHEET A.F. 25 S.W.
	28th 29th 30th 31st		1 Company training the other 3 Coys finding working parties. Draft of 10 OR found on 28th. 2nd Lieut. & 2nd Lieut Grieve to and afternoon and 1. OR wounded on 29th	"

A. Nyhne
Lieut Col.
Commanding 6th Seas Regt.

Vol 24

Confidential

War Diary.

— of —

6th (S) Bn Wiltshire Regiment

From 1st to 30th June 1917.

Volume 24

WAR DIARY
or
INTELLIGENCE SUMMARY.
(Erase heading not required.)

Army Form C. 2118.

Instructions regarding War Diaries and Intelligence Summaries are contained in F.S. Regs., Part II. and the Staff Manual respectively. Title pages will be prepared in manuscript.

Place	Date	Hour	Summary of Events and Information	Remarks and references to Appendices
	1917			
WESTON CAMP	June 1.		Battalion relieved 9th Royal Welch Fusrs in the Right sub sector of the DIEPPENDAAL Sector. "D" & "C" Companies in front line, "A" in support, "B" Company in Reserve. Night spent in preparing Assembly Trenches. 2nd Lt Avatin wounded.	MAP SHEET 28. S.N.
			Day remained at rest.	
IN THE TRENCHES	" 2		Enemy artillery active shelling our batteries in vicinity of Headquarts. Our artillery active throughout the day.	"
"	" 3		At 11am practice barrage on IV Corps front by our artillery. At 3pm practice barrage along the whole of 2d Army Front. Smoke candles were lit in front line. No retaliation by enemy. Battalion relieved by 9 Welch Regt & proceeded to MURRUMBIDGEE Camp, near to CLYTTE.	"
MURRUMBIDGEE CAMP	" 4		Day spent in generally cleaning up, baths & dressing. Issue of "Leg King" Order "Kit".	"
"	" 5		"A" & "B" Companies relieved 2 Companies of 9 Welch Regt in Right Subsector of DIEPPENDAAL Sector. One man Killed and 2 wounded during Relief.	"
			Remainder of Battalion proceeded to WESTON Camp.	
WESTON CAMP	" 6		At 9pm remainder of Battalion proceeded to Assembly Trenches. Battalion H.Q.	"

WAR DIARY
or
INTELLIGENCE SUMMARY.
(Erase heading not required.)

Army Form C. 2118.

Instructions regarding War Diaries and Intelligence Summaries are contained in F. S. Regs., Part II. and the Staff Manual respectively. Title pages will be prepared in manuscript.

Place	Date 1917 June	Hour	Summary of Events and Information	Remarks and references to Appendices
			To enemy staff in front line. Supplies removed to reinforcement camps at N.H.C. 50. 3 other ranks killed.	MAP SHEET 28 S.W.
IN THE LINE.	7.		Battalion took part in the attack and capture by 2nd Army of the MESSINES- WYCHAETE RIDGE. The Battalion was the right hand Battalion of the Right Brigade of left Division of IX Corps. At Zero-hour, 3.10 a.m., 3 men were reported on the HOLLANDSCHESCHUUR CHESCHUR Salient in immediate front of Battalion. The objective of the Battalion was the capture of the HOLLANDSCHUUR Salient in immediate front of Battalion); the S.E. portion of GRAND BOIS and consolidation of fied line. This was successfully carried out. 5 Machine guns, 3 Lewis Mortars & 179 prisoners being captured and 50 of the enemy being killed during the advance. On the capture of further objective Battalion moved forward to Green line in support. Consolidation proceeded with and pring points established.	
	8		Consolidation proceeded and work of clearing up Battlefield carried out.	
	9.		Consolidation. Cleaning up battlefield, salvaging etc. continued. At 6 p.m.	

WAR DIARY
or
INTELLIGENCE SUMMARY.
(Erase heading not required.)

Army Form C. 2118.

Instructions regarding War Diaries and Intelligence Summaries are contained in F.S. Regs., Part II. and the Staff Manual respectively. Title pages will be prepared in manuscript.

Place	Date 1917	Hour	Summary of Events and Information	Remarks and references to Appendices
			56 Brigade relieved 58 Brigade. The 6.D.L.I. moving back into Divisional Reserve in BOIS CARRÉ. Our casualties for 6, 7, 8 & 9 were Capt. Harlow wounded (who subsequently died) 2nd Lieuts Skeggs & Porter wounded. Other ranks 8 killed and 93 wounded.	MAP SHEET 28 S.W.
BOIS CARRÉ	" 10.		Day spent in resting in Rear Reserve Trench and refitting the men. Scheme forwarned. At 8.15pm Battalion moved off to relieve the 8th Buffs holding the front made from Line against Enemy in OOSTAVERNE WOOD. Barrage opened on both sides during relief. Total casualties ? Other ranks 2 killed and 10 wounded.	"
OOSTAVERNE WOOD	" 11		Relief completed at 2am and Commanding Officer toured the trenches at 4/5am. Enemy shelled all the afternoon with 5.9's, particularly Suffolk Trenches.	"
"	" 12.		GOC 58 Brigade (Commanding Officer) went round trenches at 2.30am. Enemy shelled continuously all the afternoon - 3 other ranks killed and 2 wounded.	"
"	" 13.		Heavy shelling by both sides throughout the day. Enemy was	"

WAR DIARY
OR
INTELLIGENCE SUMMARY.

(Erase heading not required.)

Army Form C. 2118.

Place	Date	Hour	Summary of Events and Information	Remarks and references to Appendices
	June			MAP SHEET 28. SH.
	" 14.		Referred to be manning 1 Battalion was ordered to "Stand to." 6 killed and 2 wounded. No attack followed	
			Enemy fairly quiet all day until 7.30pm when we made an attack on left. Enemy retaliated on our front. Relieved by 9th Cheshires	
			relief being completed by R. midnight and proceed to Camp near Hal Reserve Line. Enemy casualties Other ranks 2 killed and 3 wounded.	
	" 15.		Resting and relieving OLD Reserve Line and vicinity. Working party at night to Lape Sector. 1 man wounded.	
	" 16.		Resting and cleaning up. Working party 200 on fatigues night. Battalion ordered to "Stand to" about 9.30pm in response to S.O.S. sent up on our front.	
	" 17.		Chisel Parade. At 8/10 pm one of our planes brought down in flames - Pilot landed safely. It was reported that neither pilot or observer were personally hurt. At 9pm orders received that Battalion would be relieved next day.	

WAR DIARY
or
INTELLIGENCE SUMMARY.
(Erase heading not required.)

Army Form C. 2118.

Place	Date	Hour	Summary of Events and Information	Remarks and references to Appendices
	June			
	18.		Battalion relieved by Battalion of 5th Brigade. Proceeded to CURRAGH CAMP staying there the night. Relief completed at 9.15pm	28. S.H.
CURRAGH	19.		Battalion moved to Camp at S.2.a.7.0. near BAILLEUL on S.2.a.7.0.	
CAMP.			Coys. Keene.	cb
Mt BAILLEUL	20.		Resting.	cb
"	21.		Platoon Raining in morning – Physical Training Bayonet fighting	cb
			Instruction under S.M. FRAPE. Working Party of 51 to BAILLEUL	
			Evening. Lecture Leaders class commenced (N.C.O. per Platoon)	cb
"	22.		Brigade Parade and address by G.O.C. 58. Brigade.	cb
"	23.		Platoon Training on lines laid down in S.S. 143 "Instruction for the	cb
			Training of Platoons in Offensive Action". Sports games in the	
			afternoon. Section Leaders class continued.	cb
"	24.		Church Parade.	cb
"	25.		Platoon Training. Class of NCOs under Capt. G. PRITCHARD. –	cb
			Divisional Commanders Conference with all Commanding Officers in Camp.	cb

WAR DIARY
or
INTELLIGENCE SUMMARY.
(Erase heading not required.)

Army Form C. 2118.

Place	Date	Hour	Summary of Events and Information	Remarks and references to Appendices
N. BAILLEUL	June 26.		Platoon Training. N.Cos. Class. Divisional Horse Show.	ch. SHEET 28 SW.
	27.		Platoon Training. Recreational Training in afternoon.	62 a +0. ch.
	28.		Brigade Sports. Battalion teams 4x100 attending. Relay Race. 2nd Prize in 100 yards, 1st + 3rd Prize in the mile, 3rd Prize in High Jump and 1st Prize in inter School Lewis Race.	ab " "
	29.		Second in Command and Company Commanders to Thiéves to witness demonstration by Platoon in attack. Inspection of Brigade in afternoon by G.O.C. Division.	ab " "
	30.		Platoon Training. Lectures. Conference in Camp by G.O.C. Services with Battalion Commanders regarding.	ab " "

AS Hyland Lt Col
Comdg 6th Welsh Regt
1/7/17.

Vol - 25

6th BATTALION.
WILTSHIRE REGT.
No ......
Date ......

Confidential.

War Diary
— of —

6th (S) Bn Wiltshire Regiment.

From 1st to 31st July 1917.

Volume 25.

WAR DIARY

(Erase heading not required.)

Army Form C. 2118.

Place	Date	Hour	Summary of Events and Information	Remarks and references to Appendices
N. BAILLEUL	July 1	-	Sunday - Church Parade.	
"	2	-	Battalion moved at 5 pm and proceeded to Camp in Divisional support near KENNEL.	SHEET 28 SW. S.2 d. 7.0.
KENNEL	3	-	Resting - Platoon inspection & talks.	
"	4	-	"A" & "B" Companies Physical training & Bayonet fighting under C.S.M. Lrape -	do. SHEET 28 SW. S.23.c.
"	-	-	"C" & "D" Companies wiring instruction - H.M. the King visited Old British line in the morning.	do.
"	5	-	"A" & "B" Companies found 100 men each for work in burying cable at NORTHERN BRICKSTACK at 5 am. "C" & "D" Companies wiring instruction and physical training and Bayonet fighting under C.S.M. Lrape.	"
"	6	-	Working party as in previous day but found by "C" & "D" Companies. "A" & "B" Companies practising rapid wiring - recreational training.	"
"	7	-	Working party continued - found by "A" & "B" Companies. "C" & "D" Companies wiring instruction - Signallers & Scouts exercises under Lieut Lowe.	" do.
"	8	-	Sunday - "C" & "D" Companies on working party - Remained in Church Parade.	do.
"	9	-	"A" & "B" Companies on working party - G.O.C. 58 Infantry Brigade witnessed.	do.

Army Form C. 2118.

WAR DIARY

(Erase heading not required.)

Instructions regarding War Diaries and Intelligence Summaries are contained in F. S. Regs., Part II. and the Staff Manual respectively. Title pages will be prepared in manuscript.

Place	Date	Hour	Summary of Events and Information	Remarks and references to Appendices
Nr KEMMEL	July 9		During demonstration by "C" Company - "D" Company accompanied. Telephone training.	SHEET 28 SW
	" 10		Battalion relieved 10th Royal Warwickshire Regiment in Brigade Support - Headquarters at the DAMMSTRASSE. O.9.c.2.9. "A" Company at GOUDEZEUNE FARM. 0.15.b.0.4. -	WYTSCHAETE
			"B" Company at DELSEKE. 0.16.c.3.3. "C" Coy in OBOE TRENCH. 0.10.a. "D" Company in PHEASANT WOOD O.9.b.	a.b.
DAMMSTRASSE	" 11.		Battalion relieved 8th North Staffs Regt in front line from about O.11.C.4.10 to O.17.a.2.1. "A","B","C" Companies in front line. "D" Coy in support in ROSE WOOD. O.16.a. Headquarters in DENYS WOOD. O.9.a.4.5.	" a.b.
IN THE TRENCHES.	" 12		Our artillery active throughout the day - Enemy shelled RAVINE WOOD and DENYS WOOD at night - some gas shells were also sent over. 1 man wounded.	" a.b.
"	" 13.		Our artillery active - Enemy artillery shelled heavily during the night of 13/14. - Major Tynan & 050 wounded but remained at duty. 1 man wounded.	" a.b.
"	" 14		2 Other ranks killed. 17 wounded. 2nd Lt Langley wounded.	" a.b.
"	" 15		Battalion relieved by 9th Br Royal Welsh Fusiliers and proceeded to dugouts in	" a.b.

WAR DIARY

Army Form C. 2118.

(Erase heading not required.)

Instructions regarding War Diaries and Intelligence Summaries are contained in F. S. Regs., Part II. and the Staff Manual respectively. Title pages will be prepared in manuscript.

Place	Date	Hour	Summary of Events and Information	Remarks and references to Appendices
	July 15		Brigade Support. Disposition of Companies the same as on 10th instant. Headquarters remaining in DENYS WOOD. 1 Man wounded during relief.	WYTSCHAETE 1/10,000
			Bombs were dropped on transport during the night - wounding 1 man	a.g.
			Grenades 3 killed & 1 wounded.	
DENYS WOOD	"		Being this turn in the trenches a great deal of work was done in	
			improving the enemy dug trenches and digging new trenches & communications	"
			up with them already dug not on either side.	
"	" 16		Working party of 150 found for work on new Communication trench - Enemy	
			shelled DENYS WOOD and vicinity of billets during the evening - Our	
			artillery very active.	a.g.
"	" 17		9th Cheshire Regiment in front line shelled JUNCTION BUILDINGS in enemy	1
			lines. Enemy artillery shelled DENYS WOOD heavily in vicinity of Headquarters.	
			100 Other ranks found for work on new communication trench.	"
"	" 18		Battalion relieved by 7th Loyal North Lancs Regt. Proceeded to DONCASTER	28 S.H.
			HUTS N. LOCRE - relief completed about 5am on 19?	a.g. M.23.c.
N. LOCRE	" 19		Resting generally cleaning up. "C" & "D" Companies bathing in afternoon	a.g. "

A1945. Wt. W11422/M1160 350,000 12/16 D.D.& L. Forms/C2118/14

WAR DIARY

Army Form C. 2118.

Place	Date	Hour	Summary of Events and Information	Remarks and references to Appendices
N. LOCRE	July 20	-	Reorganisation. Cleaning up. - Baths in afternoon.	a/c SHEET 28 SW M.23.C.
"	21	-	Platoon training. - Arm. drill etc.	a/c
"	22	-	Sunday - Church Parade.	
"	23	-	Physical Training - Bayonet fighting - Musketry - Lt specimen attacked about 4/30pm & dropping bombs, killing 4 animals wounding 4.	
"			Bombs were dropped on Transport lines - killing 4 animals wounding	a/c
"			4 other ranks wounded.	
"	24	-	These days were spent in training from 9am - 1pm. Physical Training -	a/c
"	25	-	Bayonet fighting, Platoon training - Musketry firing on range - Signallers &	
"	26	-	entrained under 2/Lt Granger - Lewis training under 2/Lt Liley - C.Col.Off.	"
"	27	-	Lost R.S. Symons R.S.O. left over temporary Command of 58 Brigade on 27th during Offr.	a/c
"	28		Enemy shown by Brigade Lieut. Ellason RSO.	"
"	29	-	Sunday - Church Parade - Battalion relieved Kings own Lancs Regt	"
"			in divisional support near Ravine at B.23.c.oo on 2nd in-letter.	a/c
"	30	-	Day spent in equipping men & in fighting order - Battalion moved at 8/30pm	"
			to assembly position near ESTAMINET CORNER O.H.C. Surplus personnel to	
			SIEGE FARM. A draft of 5 other ranks joined.	"

WAR DIARY

(Erase heading not required.)

Army Form C. 2118.

Place	Date	Hour	Summary of Events and Information	Remarks and references to Appendices
N°. STANINET CORNER.	July 31		Remained in Assembly position. Casualties - 1 Man killed 12 wounded.	MAP SHEET 28. S.W.2
			A. Thynne Lt-Col	
			Comg. 6th Welch Regiment.	

Vol 26

Confidential

War Diary

— of —

6"(S) B". Wiltshire Regiment.

From 30" July 1917 to 31" August 1917.

Volume 26.

WAR DIARY
or
INTELLIGENCE SUMMARY.
(Erase heading not required.)

Army Form C. 2118.

Place	Date	Hour	Summary of Events and Information	Remarks and references to Appendices
IN THE TRENCHES	30.7.17 (contd)	—	Battalion marched up to ridge opposite about ESTAMINET CORNER – "C" & "D" Coys in front	WYTSCHAETE 5A
			Sent "A" & "C" Coys on outpost line. Battalion was in support to 56th Brigade. One man killed and 2 wounded.	N.
"	31.7.17 (contd)	—	Third Battle of YPRES. Zero hour 3.50 a.m. Battalion in support to 56th Brigade	"
			and advanced in attack on the BLUE LINE, East of GREEN WOOD – JUNCTION BUILDINGS –	
			Odense Barrage – Allges Relocation in support area chiefly about OOSTAVERNE	
			WOOD. Heavy rain night of 31/1.º	a.s.
"	1.8.17		Remained in support 2inches all day and relieved 7th Kings Own Lancs Regt in	3
			Right out sector. "C" Company left front, "D" Company right front. "B" Company	1
			in close support. "A" Company in Reserve. Headquarters. POLKA ESTAMINET.	
			Orders to counter attack position retaken by enemy. Attack postponed until	"
			following night. Our line advanced on Right by peaceful penetration about	
			100 yards and line of posts established.	2f
"	2.8.17		Heavy rain continued. Lost 1 Lewis in boot area. Attack under barrage	"
			further postponed but our line further advanced on under Battalion front	
			during night 2/3 rd about 200 yards and new line of posts established.	4

WAR DIARY
or
INTELLIGENCE SUMMARY.
(Erase heading not required.)

Army Form C. 2118.

Place	Date	Hour	Summary of Events and Information	Remarks and references to Appendices
IN THE TRENCHES.	3.8.17	—	Men much exhausted and suffering owing to deplorable condition of trenches. Night of 3/4th relieved in right sub sector by 9. Cheshire Regiment. Casualties while holding the line Capt. C. Buckland slightly wounded but remained at duty. Other ranks 4 killed, 16 wounded and 1 missing. Battalion moved to Brigade Support area. "A" & "B" Coys to MAUVE LINE. "C" 1·D" Coys to RIDGE DEFENCES. Headquarters to ONRAET WOOD. Lots relief.	WYTSCHAETE 5A
"	4.8.17		Resting — Ageing clothes. 23 NCOs & Men evacuated sick chiefly through exhaustion & exposure.	a9
"	5.8.17		30 more NCOs & men evacuated sick, majority of cases caused through exposure. Relieved 9 Cheshire Regiment in right subsector. Battalion punch strength 302 other ranks. "B" Company left front. "A" Company right front. "D" Company in close support. "C" Coy in reserve. Relief delayed on account of heavy barrage. S.O.S. being sent up on left front and taken on right front. Casualties during relief half Dawson wounded & 10 other ranks wounded. Owing to barrage on both sides it was impossible to proceed much further with consolidating the line taken over.	a9

Army Form C. 2118.

WAR DIARY
or
INTELLIGENCE SUMMARY.
(Erase heading not required.)

Instructions regarding War Diaries and Intelligence Summaries are contained in F. S. Regs., Part II and the Staff Manual respectively. Title pages will be prepared in manuscript.

Place	Date	Hour	Summary of Events and Information	Remarks and references to Appendices
IN THE TRENCHES	6.8.17	—	Various shelling by enemy especially around Headquarters POLKA ESTAMINET – Casualties this day 2 Other Ranks killed and 11 wounded.	WYTSCHAETE O.S. 5A.
	7.8.17	—	Battalion relieved night of 7/8th by 11th Royal Warwickshire Regt 37th Division and proceeded in Motor Lorries to Camp near BAILLEUL at S.2.a.40. (Sheet 28 SW).	o.S. 2.a 40. o.S.(Sheet 28 SW)
			Battalion arriving in camp at about 5.15 am on morning of 8th. No casualties during relay.	o.S.
M. BAILLEUL	8.8.17		Remainder of day resting.	o.S.
	9.8.17		Resting and generally cleaning up — Platoon inspection	o.S. 2.a+o.
"	10.8.17		Battalion moved from Camp and entrained at BAILLEUL at 8.30 pm.	o.S.(Sheet 28 SW)
"	11.8.17		Detrained at WIZERNES at 1am and marched to "Allies" at SENINGHEM on LUMBRES training area.	o.S.
SENINGHEM.	12.8.17		Sunday. Church Parade. 2nd Lt Mellership from 3rd W.Lks. joined	o.S. HAZEBROUCK 5A.
"	13.8.17		Monday. Platoon training — Regimental training of Reserve Signallers Scouts Snipers. L.C.O. class from 3rd W.Lks. joined.	o.S.
"	14.8.17		Training as on 13th. A draft of 80 Other Ranks joined — Marti all 6ft W.Lks men. Lt. R.H. Rose from 3rd W.Lks joined	o.S. " "

WAR DIARY
or
INTELLIGENCE SUMMARY.
(Erase heading not required.)

Army Form C. 2118.

Instructions regarding War Diaries and Intelligence Summaries are contained in F.S. Regs., Part II. and the Staff Manual respectively. Title pages will be prepared in manuscript.

Place	Date	Hour	Summary of Events and Information	Remarks and references to Appendices
SERINGHEM	1.8.17	-	Sacred Parade near HARLETTES. Presentation of medal ribbons by B.O.C. 19th Division.	HAZEBROUCK eg. 5A.
"	2.8.17	-	Company Platoon training – Musketry – Bayonet fighting – instruction under Sergeant McLeod from D Army School. Brigade Cross Country race in evening – 9th Cheshire winning – 6th Wilts second.	"
"	6.8.17	-	Brigade Sports, Battalion winning the 100 yds ¼ mile races and first in long jump. "B" Company firing on range	2/34. 2/34.
"	19.8.17	-	Sunday. Church Parade.	"
"	20.8.17	-	Divisional Sports. "D" Company on range.	2/34.
"	21.8.17	-	Platoon training – Musketry – Bayonet fighting, Instructor – Divisional Revr. to Bri races. Roll of Q.M. Kendall from Details joined.	2/34. 2/34.
"	22.8.17	-	Divisional Tactical Exercise near HARLETTES which all available officers attended.	1/34.
"	-	-	Training continued – show of NCO's under Regimental Sergeant Major. 30 extra rounds fired.	1/34.
"	23.8.17	-	"C" Company firing on range – Day wet day.	"
"	24.8.17	-	Brigade Parade for exchange of Cards for inspection by Commander.	"

WAR DIARY
INTELLIGENCE SUMMARY.
(Erase heading not required.)

Army Form C. 2118.

Instructions regarding War Diaries and Intelligence Summaries are contained in F. S. Regs., Part II. and the Staff Manual respectively. Title pages will be prepared in manuscript.

Place	Date	Hour	Summary of Events and Information	Remarks and references to Appendices
SENINGHEM				HAZEBROUCK
"	25.8.17		Inspection of Division by Commander in Chief near HARLETTES.	54.
"	26.8.17		Sunday - Route March + Church Parade.	
"	27.8.17		"A" + "C" Companies practising Platoon for attack against Shell hole defences under G.O.C. 58 Infantry Brigade. "B" + "D" Companies training.	
"	28.8.17		Battalion moved from SENINGHEM at 7.40 am entraining at WIZERNES MAP SHEET 27-28. for BAILLEUL - arrived BAILLEUL at about 3.40 pm and marched to billets near BERTHEN - around R.23.b and R.18.c (MAP sheet 27.28) at a depth of 25 other Ranks joined.	
"	29.8.17		Company training - Arm drill etc. Resting.	
"	30.8.17		Company training - Arm drill etc.	
"	31.8.17		Company training - Company in attack - Senior + NCO's class - Lectures - Musketry instruction.	
	31.8.17			

Commanding 6 Wiltshire Regt

58/19
Vol 27

Confidential

War Diary

of

6(s) Bn Wiltshire Regt.

From 1st to 30 Sept 1917.

Volume 27

WAR DIARY
or
INTELLIGENCE SUMMARY.
(Erase heading not required.)

Army Form C. 2118.

Place	Date	Hour	Summary of Events and Information	Remarks and references to Appendices
Nt BERTHEN	Sept 1/17		Company training including tactical schemes for attack on steel Pill boxes.	Sheet 28 R 18.c.
"	2nd		Sunday - Church Parade 2/Lt B.H. IVSON Rev. 3rd W.Fus. joined	A13.4
"	3rd 4 5th 6th		Company training - Class of NCOs instructed daily under Regimental Sergt Major - Senior NCO's class under 2/Lt Rangers comprising instruction in Musketry, Lewis Guns Lectures.	" A13.4
"	7.		Battalion Cross Country Run - Draft of 50 other ranks joined	" A13.4
"	8		Company training - Rocketing attack against steel Pill boxes	" A13.4
"	9.		Sunday. Church Parade. Battalion practised new method of attack in the afternoon.	A13.4
"	10.		38 Brigade regrouped into Composite Battalion. Composite Battalion of 6." Week being "C." Coy 6 arise. "A" 175" Coy's 9 m.ch.. and "6. 6y 9." Cheshire Regt. "D" Coy 6" W.Fus. forming part of composite Battalion of 9 m.ch. A & B Coys 6 W.Fus. forming part of Composite Bn of 9 Cheshire Regt. Composite Battalion of 6 W.Fus. moved to camp at N.15c.	Sheet 28 SW N 15 c. 6 A13.4

N.15c. (BEAVER CAMP) Nr. KEMMEL

September 1917 - Sheet 1.

WAR DIARY
or
INTELLIGENCE SUMMARY.
(Erase heading not required.)

Army Form C. 2118.

Place	Date 1917 Sept.	Hour	Summary of Events and Information	Remarks and references to Appendices
Mt KEMMEL	11.		Composite Battalion of 6th W.Yorks moved to SPOIL BANK at 2.30pm	ZILLEBEKE C.24
SPOIL BANK.	12.		Reconnaissance made of our front line and sunken of enemy lines	I 33a O.13.4
"	13.		Working parties	
"	14.		Battalion relieved by 13 K.R.R. and proceeded to "C" Camp at N.21a. N²KEMMEL. Sheet 28	N 21 a
Mt KEMMEL	15.		Company training. 2/Lt F.C. Blanchard & Afondeen from Scottish joined. A draft of 27 Other ranks arrived.	R.18.4 C.13.4
"	16.		Sunday - Church Parade	"
"	17.		Three 2 days spent on equipping Companies with fighting kit. Battalion split up on 18th into Composite Battalion - "C" & "D" Coys with 1 Company	
"	18.		of Cheshire and 1 Company of Welsh and Battalion Headquarters under O.C. Welsh Regt forming one Battalion - A & B Coys being attached to 1 Cheshire Welsh and remaining at ROSSIGNOL WOOD Battalion under command of O.C. Cheshire Regt. proceeded at 8pm to Entrenchment trenches N.E. of HOLLEBEKE (being conveyed by bus) from KEMMEL to ESTAMINET CORNER) taking over from 111 Brigade 2 Platoons of "A" & "C" Coys took over posts even of their respective Battns.	"

September 1917 SHEET 2.

WAR DIARY
or
INTELLIGENCE SUMMARY.

(Erase heading not required.)

Army Form C. 2118.

Place	Date	Hour	Summary of Events and Information	Remarks and references to Appendices
			front and were responsible for making all preliminary arrangements for Nosemby. The remainder of these 2 Companies were located in TRIANGULAR BLUFF under L Shapland and were responsible for completing Battalion dumps of wire, water and rescue stores in the EMBANKMENT. A string line of outposts was thrown out on South side of OPAQUE WOOD to screen the preparations. Practice Barrage at 7.30 am and 3.30 am — slight retaliation by enemy.	
IN THE TRENCHES	19th		A & B Coys formed at midnight 19/20 and joined up in assembly positions about OPAQUE WOOD. Although shell holes, broken strands of wire and fallen trees made OPAQUE WOOD a difficult obstacle to traverse, the proximity of the barrage line and the possibility of the enemy locating Coys discovering unusual movement rendered it inadvisable to assemble South of Wood. It was therefore decided to assemble in file along direction tape running S. through the WOOD and to deploy on emerging into the normal form of attack with each company in 4 lines.	

197. September Sheet No 3

Army Form C. 2118.

WAR DIARY
or
INTELLIGENCE SUMMARY.
(Erase heading not required.)

Instructions regarding War Diaries and Intelligence Summaries are contained in F. S. Regs., Part II. and the Staff Manual respectively. Title pages will be prepared in manuscript.

Place	Date	Hour	Summary of Events and Information	Remarks and references to Appendices
	1917 Sept			
	19th		The plan worked well but owing to the marshy and broken nature of the ground in front of OPAQUE WOOD the deployment posed a more difficult problem matter than was anticipated. The EMBANKMENT Land beding to Assembly positions was packed with troops and there was some promiscuous shelling and the night was very dark and had the ground been heavy the Assembly could never have been completed in time. The success of the Assembly was largely due to the careful reconnaissance by M. Evans carried out by each Platoon leader concerned. B.H.	
OPAQUE WOOD	20th		The Battalion formed the right flank in the attack by the 2nd and 3rd Armies on the MENIN Road approaching ridges having the GWELTE on left and 2nd Bedfords (3? Division) on its W. front of count on the right the objectives of the Batln were as follows — A Company right assaulting Company, C Company left Assaulting Company, B Company right support, D Company left support — Boundaries between Companies the bell running S.E. by S. from OPAQUE WOOD.	

September 1917. Sheet No 4.

WAR DIARY
or
INTELLIGENCE SUMMARY.

Army Form C. 2118.

Place	Date	Hour	Summary of Events and Information	Remarks and references to Appendices
	20.		The belt inclusive to Left Company. Carrying Party and Battalion forward command Post in rear. Battalion Battle HQr on N.E. side	
of Embankment BATTLE WOOD			At Zero hour 5.40 a.m. Battalion advanced to the attack under a heavy Creeping Barrage by our Artillery. Left front company met with little opposition except for continuous Machine Gun fire from the direction of CEMETERY EMBANKMENT. The machine guns appear to be located beyond the objective line and to fire through the Barrage. The dugouts in the wood at about O.6.d.7.7. were dealt with 3 Germans being killed and 19 taken prisoner. On 'D' Coy on the right assumed to meet with considerable resistance. Capt. WILLIAMS (O.C. 'C' Coy) ordered his right front Lewis Gun to open a brisk fire on the dugouts in front of that company. On the left the 9th Welch did not reach their objective until 30 minutes after 'C' Coy had begun consolidating. to cover his left flank Capt. Williams formed a defensive flank of posts and asked for assistance.	

September 1917 – Sheet 5.

WAR DIARY
or
INTELLIGENCE SUMMARY.
(Erase heading not required.)

Army Form C. 2118.

Place	Date	Hour	Summary of Events and Information	Remarks and references to Appendices
	20.		Five fops from the left hear platoon were subsequently met between when the 9" pltct came up. The Company reached its objective 06a.75.65 – 06a.37. within 37 minutes of Zero and flares were lit in response to aeroplane calls at Zero plus 42. The consolidation was covered by Lewis Guns and the Company snipers who were busily engaged endeavouring to pick off Germans moving down the Railway Embankment and also in keeping down enemy snipers on the immediate left. One platoon under Lieut. remained posted in a forward position from the morning of the 20th until relieved on the night 21/22. Left Support Company consolidated its portion of the intermediate line several casualties were caused by sniping. The ground was very wet and water logged in places but posns were formed with sandbags. On different occasions our platoon was moved up to assist the left front Company before a different flank before the 9 L. Weals had come into touch and later as our reinforce. September 1917. Sheet No. 6	

WAR DIARY
or
INTELLIGENCE SUMMARY.
(Erase heading not required).

Army Form C. 2118.

Place	Date	Hour	Summary of Events and Information	Remarks and references to Appendices
	1917 Sept 20.		by a second platoon with orders to disperse vigorously against HESSIAN WOOD which was then believed to be holding up Q_4th. A battle patrol was sent out from the Company when the barrage lifted. Although is discovered no enemy on the immediate front of the objective, it came across a bombing post recently evacuated and some considerable shell hole with arm shelters destroyed by artillery fire. On the 27th this section of the entire stock line was harassed by enemy snipers who made commensurate offensive — it was also subjected to considerable shell fire. The enemy apparently photog by direct observation. All officers of Right front Coy were killed or attaining their objectives therefore the only authentic information came from N.C.Os. On the entrenchment the attack was pushed well forward and a post established beyond the actual objective. This post was held until relief on the night 21/22 although at times heavily shelled. Touch was maintained with the 2 Bedfords on the right near the	

September 1917 — Sheet 7. |

WAR DIARY
or
INTELLIGENCE SUMMARY.

(Erase heading not required.)

Army Form C. 2118.

Place	Date	Hour	Summary of Events and Information	Remarks and references to Appendices
	20.		to the East of the Embankment Capt Langley led the attack upon the dugouts. Sgt GRAVES Capa After the man killed the right section of his party took up position in shell holes S. of the Copse and dug in at dusk. The left of the party which had reached the side of the CEMETERY found the ground in the immediate front broken and wet and without a field of fire – the N.C.O. in charge withdrew them to the N. side of the Cemetery to obtain a better field of fire. The movement appears to have been carried out in an orderly manner back a line of posts dug in a semi-circle, the left on lines with "C" Coy but the right flank "in the air" altogether covering the right front by the advanced posts. The right support Company had a clear way to go and they began digging the intermediate line before it was sufficiently light to recognise the landmarks previously reconnoitred with the result that when it became light the position had to	

September 1917   Sheet 8.

Army Form C. 2118.

WAR DIARY
or
INTELLIGENCE SUMMARY.
(Erase heading not required.)

Instructions regarding War Diaries and Intelligence Summaries are contained in F. S. Regs., Part II. and the Staff Manual respectively. Title pages will be prepared in manuscript.

Place	Date	Hour	Summary of Events and Information	Remarks and references to Appendices
	20.		He noticed throughout the day they were hotted by snipers from tops front and Machine Gun fire from Right front. A little patrol was sent out but came under considerable Machine Gun fire and suffered several casualties. Subsequently two platoons were moved to the Entrenchment which at was considered advisable to hold in greater strength and covered the whole of the valley towards HESSIAN WOOD. Harping parties executed such lines of wire and craters behind rest of the supporting troops as when they followed through but sniping and Machine Gun fire made it impossible for them to work in daylight.	
	20/21		Consolidation continued during night of 20/21. Surplus personnel of officers repines. Lt. BONE taking command of B Coy & 2 Lt. Blanchard repining D Coy. Lieut Kent remaining as Battalion Headquarters and Major Tynan O.C.O. at Brigade H.Q. Wth	
	1/22		Battalion relieved night of 21/22 by 7th Kings Own Lancs Regt	

September 1917 — Sheet 9.

WAR DIARY
or
INTELLIGENCE SUMMARY.
(Erase heading not required.)

Army Form C. 2118.

Place	Date	Hour	Summary of Events and Information	Remarks and references to Appendices
			and proceeded to Camp N^r KEMMEL N 21 C – The casualties for this show were – Capt PH Williams, Capt A. Langley, Lieut A.L. Hopeland, 2/Lt F.L. Savage killed, 2/Lt W.T. Graiger died of wounds. Capt G. Buckland wounded. Other ranks were 24 killed, 4 died of wounds, 5 missing and 113 wounded. Total 146.	SHEET 28. "
	23rd		Battalion remained at Camp getting under afternoon when it moved to Camp at BOIS CONFLUENT.	SHEET 23 28 SW.
BOIS CONFLUENT.	24 25		Battalion proceeded to SPOIL BANK on 24th. Working party of 200 found during RE Material nights of 24/25. Afternoon of 25th Battalion relieved by 8 East Lancs Regt proceeded to Camp on North side of BOIS CARRÉ.	ZILLEBEKE I 33 Z. SHEET 28 SW N 62.
BOIS CARRÉ	26		Resting – Drafts of 233 other ranks joined from Royal Wilts Yeomanry.	
"	27 28		Platoon drill Company inspections. Training and Drill Experiments with New Box Light Water Kirkel Squile.	

September 1917. Sheet 10.

WAR DIARY
or
INTELLIGENCE SUMMARY.
(Erase heading not required.)

Army Form C. 2118.

Place	Date	Hour	Summary of Events and Information	Remarks and references to Appendices
BOIS CARRÉE	29		Battalion moved from camp at BOIS CARRÉE - Headquarters, A & B Companies to SPOIL BANK - C & D Coys to BOIS CONFLUENT.	A.B. LILLEBEKE I 33 b 28
			Working party of 50 found carrying R.E. material -	
	30		Working party of 50 men on pioneer night	
			The following Officers from 1st Royal Welsh Yeomanry joined on 26th - Major L.S. Awdry.	
			Major W. Taller, Lieutenants J. Megaw, L.N. Bagg, M.L. Lunnon, R.C. Lotz.	
			Lieutenants H.S. Lignon, R.E.N. Hawkings, I.F.P. Bacon, Lt. E.G. Lamor.	
			Lieutenant Bernard Kingston Powell, 2/Lt. Geo. C. Harrison, L.C. Edwards, and	
			A.C. Sighs.	
			Total Strength of Battalion to 30.9.17, 46 Officers and 1040 Other ranks.	

V. Wynne Major
Army Welshmen Regt

58/9
Vol 28

Confidential

War Diary
— of —
6 (S) B? Wiltshire Reg?

From 1st to 31st October 1917.

Volume 28

Army Form C. 2118.

WAR DIARY
or
INTELLIGENCE SUMMARY.
(Erase heading not required.)

Instructions regarding War Diaries and Intelligence Summaries are contained in F. S. Regs., Part II. and the Staff Manual respectively. Title pages will be prepared in manuscript.

Place	Date 1917	Hour	Summary of Events and Information	Remarks and references to Appendices
SPOIL BANK	Oct 1. & 2.	-	Working parties supplies for carrying tools these days.	ZILLEBEKE I.33.d.
"	" 3	-	Battalion relieved 9" Welch in right sub sector. - A.B.C. Companies on front line - Don Support - Battalion H.Q. in the EMBANKMENT.	"
IN THE TRENCHES	" 4	-	Enemy at intervals during the day shelled our front line of posts. Work on posts & entanglements was continued and some strongpoints were erected. Casualties 2 other ranks killed and 3 O.R. wounded.	I.36.C. "
"	" 5 & " 6	-	Enemy artillery quiet. - Own artillery carried out practice barrage during both days. Work on entanglements posts & trenches continued.	" "
"	" 7	-	Battalion relieved in line by 9" Welch and proceeded to dugouts in Brigade Reserve - A & B Coys HQR to SPOIL BANK. C & D Coys to BUFFS BANK and GASPERS CLIFF respectively. 2 other ranks wounded during relief.	"
SPOIL BANK	" 8	-	Working party of 100 other ranks carrying timber for forward work.	I.33.d.
"	" 9	-	Working party as previous day. - Battalion relieved 9" Welch Regt as in Brigade - A.B. & D in front line - "C" Coy in support - HQR in the EMBANKMENT. Whilst relief was in progress enemy shelled junction of OAF TRENCH and the EMBANKMENT. 3 Other Ranks being killed and 4 wounded.	"
"	" 10	-	Line of posts 1 Battalion M.G. shelled at intervals during the day. Casualties 1 other Rank	I.36.C.

October 1917. Sheet 1.

WAR DIARY
or
INTELLIGENCE SUMMARY.
(Erase heading not required.)

Army Form C. 2118.

Instructions regarding War Diaries and Intelligence Summaries are contained in F. S. Regs., Part II. and the Staff Manual respectively. Title pages will be prepared in manuscript.

Place	Date 1917	Hour	Summary of Events and Information	Remarks and references to Appendices
ROSSIGNOL CAMP.	Oct 10	-	Rested and Cleaned.	VILLEBERT a/b I 36c
"	" 11	-	Battalion relieved by 8' Gloucester Regt and proceeded to ROSSIGNOL CAMP.	a/b Sheet 28 SW
"	" 12	-	Resting, cleaning equipment. Lewis Guns. Camp.	a/b N 32c
"	" 13	-	Company training.	a/b "
"	" 14	-	250 Other ranks transferred to Base. Draft of 30 other ranks joined. 6th being distributed by 66 c D Division & G.O.C. Brigade	a/b "
"	" 15	-	Reorganisation.	a/b "
"	" 16	-	Platoon training - Class of NCOs under Regimental Sergeant Major - 2/Lt S.S. Heller Gen.	a/b "
"	" 17	-	3rd/4th joined together with a draft of 91 other ranks.	a/b "
"	" 18	-	Platoon training - Class of NCO's under Regimental Sergeant Major.	a/b "
"	" 19	-	Battalion moved to SPOIL BANK relieving 10" Worcesters. A & C Coys T.M.B. in tunnels on North side of Canal. B Company in tunnel south side of Canal. D Coy in GASPARD CLIFF. Bomb dropped at Aleut 6pm in transport Lines. 1 Other rank killed & 3 Wounded.	a/b "
SPOIL BANK	20 & 21 & 22	-	SPOIL BANK fairly shelled. Working parties - cleaning up tunnels - saturing bombs etc.	a/b "

October 1917. Sheet 2.

Army Form C. 2118.

WAR DIARY
or
INTELLIGENCE SUMMARY.
(Erase heading not required.)

Instructions regarding War Diaries and Intelligence Summaries are contained in F. S. Regs., Part II. and the Staff Manual respectively. Title pages will be prepared in manuscript.

Place	Date 1917	Hour	Summary of Events and Information	Remarks and references to Appendices
SPOIL BANK	Oct 23/24	—	Battalion relieved 9 Welch on Line A.C. & 9 boys in front line – Line running from BELGIAN WOOD to CANAL. Quiet relief. 8 Coy in Support – N.B. 1st Embankment. Lieut N.R. Grigson from Royal Wiltshire Yeomanry joined.	ZILLEBEKE I.3.b.c.
IN THE TRENCHES	" 24	—	OAF Trench (communicating trench) shelled heavily during morning – quiet afternoon and evening.	"
"	" 25	—	EMBANKMENT shelled all day – very heavy at 5pm.	"
"	" 26	—	General attack from Ypres on left, Northwards – our troops on left shelled – no damage. Company HQ. shelled fairly during morning and afternoon. 2/Lt S.H. Williams from 3rd Wilts joined. Strength of 67 other ranks joined.	"
"	27/28	—	EMBANKMENT and Communicating Trenches freely shelled morning and afternoon. Battalion relieved by Loyal North Lancs and proceeded to Camp N. BRASSERIE. Relief complete by 7.15pm. Casualties during this tour in trenches were 4 other ranks wounded.	Sheet 28 S.W. N.8.e.35.
N. BRASSERIE	28 } 29 } 30 } 31 }		Resting – baths. Platoon Training – Improvement to fields etc. 2/Lt. B.H. Dixon transferred to 2/5 Welsh Regt on 28. Lt. Neale & 2/Lt S.S. Meller transferred to 2/o Berkshire and 2. CR. Wells, 2/Lt Jenkin R. 2/Lt Ott transferred to 1/4 Wilts 22.10.17. Lieut Kersey from Royal Wilts Yeomanry joined.	"

A.J. Trypane Lt Col
COMMANDING 6th SERVICE Bn. WILTSHIRE REGIMENT.

Vol 29

Confidential

War Diary
of
6(S) Wiltshire Regiment

From 1st to 30th Nov. 1917.

Volume 29.

6TH WILTSHIRE REGT.

WAR DIARY
or
INTELLIGENCE SUMMARY.

(Erase heading not required.)

Army Form C. 2118.

Instructions regarding War Diaries and Intelligence Summaries are contained in F. S. Regs., Part II. and the Staff Manual respectively. Title pages will be prepared in manuscript.

Place	Date	Hour	Summary of Events and Information	Remarks and references to Appendices
N. ROSSIGNOL	Nov 1	-	Working Parties - Generally improving camp	SHEET 28 SW
"	" 2	-	Working Parties - Spoil Boards & Trenches	a.d.
"	" 3	-	Working Parties - do	a.d.
"	" 4	-	Working Parties - do	a.d.
"	" 5	-	Battalion moved to ROSSIGNOL CAMP Nr. KEMMEL - Working Parties to Forward area	a.d.
"	" 6	-	Platoon Training - Drafts of 16 other ranks joined.	a.d.
ROSSIGNOL CAMP	" 7	-	Platoon Training - Section Leaders Class - Lewis Beams, Smoke Ferrets from	a.d.
"	" 8	-	3rd Battalion joined on 8?	a.d.
"	" 9	-	Battalion moved to Attach in STRAZEELE	a.d.
STRAZEELE	" 10	-	Resting - Draft of 45 other ranks joined	a.d. HAZEBROUCK 5A.
"	" 11	-	Battalion moved to LYNDE in BLARINGHEM Training Area	a.d.
LYNDE	" 12	-	Resting	a.d.
"	" 13	-	Company Training - NCOs under Regimental Sergeant Major	MAP SHEET 36 A
"	" 14	-	Platoon Training - Section Leaders Class Assembled - Class of NCOs under Regt Sergt Major	B.5.6. a.d.

WAR DIARY
INTELLIGENCE SUMMARY.
(Erase heading not required.)

Army Form C. 2118.

Place	Date	Hour	Summary of Events and Information	Remarks and references to Appendices
LYNDE	15/16		Platoon training - Lecturers Class - Musical Classes of Instruction	SHEET 36A
"	17		under Regimental Sergt Major. Sigs. of 2 other ranks joined on 17th	"
"			Working party for work on range found on 17th	"
"	18		Sunday - Voluntary Church Parade. Working party for range.	"
"	19		Training Continued - Musical Classes of Instruction - Recreational training	"
"	20		in afternoon.	"
"	21		Working parties for work on range took these days - training -	"
"	22		Football Cross Country runs in afternoon.	"
"	23		Sunday - Battalion Cross Country Run.	"
"	24		Training - Class of N.C.O.s under Regimental Sergt Major. L.O.C.'s	"
"	25		inspection of Transport on 25th.	"
"	26		Training - Lewis Gunners firing on range.	"
"	27		More training continued	"
"	28		2 L A.C. Band from 3rd W.R. Joined.	"
"	29		Medal Presentation to 58 Brigade by G.O.C. 19th Division - Brigade Parade on Cross	"
			County Run in afternoon which Batlk won	"

NOVR 1917 Sheet 2.

Army Form C. 2118.

WAR DIARY
or
INTELLIGENCE SUMMARY.
(Erase heading not required.)

Instructions regarding War Diaries and Intelligence Summaries are contained in F. S. Regs., Part II. and the Staff Manual respectively. Title pages will be prepared in manuscript.

Place	Date	Hour	Summary of Events and Information	Remarks and references to Appendices
LYNDE	Nov 30.		500 West ponds proceeded to CORMETTE for musketry - Remainder staying at LYNDE.	

J.T. Lyne an Mayr 2/Lt-Col
COMMANDING 2nd SERVICE Bn. WILTSHIRE REGIMENT.

Confidential.

War Diary

of

6th Wiltshire Regiment

From 1st to 31st December 1917.

Volume 30.

WAR DIARY
or
INTELLIGENCE SUMMARY.
(Erase heading not required.)

Army Form C. 2118.

Instructions regarding War Diaries and Intelligence Summaries are contained in F. S. Regs., Part II. and the Staff Manual respectively. Title pages will be prepared in manuscript.

Place	Date 1917 Dec	Hour	Summary of Events and Information	Remarks and references to Appendices
TILQUES	1	-	Being on Range	-
"	2	-	Being on Range – Battalion relieved for four moves to LYNDE in evening.	HAZEBROUCK 54
LYNDE	3	-	Lewis Guns firing at Range at TILQUES – Company training – Recreational training in afternoon	"
"	4	-	"	"
"	5	-	"	
"	6	-	"	
"	7	-	Battalion left LYNDE – entraining at ARQUES Station – A.B.C. & HQ. entraining at 12.27 pm – D Company at 8.57 pm. Detained at BEAUMETZ – A.B.C. & HQ at 10.15 pm – D Coy detraining at 6 am on 8th. Marched to Camp at BLAIRVILLE.	"
BLAIRVILLE	8	-	Battalion marched to Camp near GOMMECOURT.	"
GOMMECOURT	9	-	Battalion left GOMMECOURT at 7.40 am and marched to Camp near ETRICOURT.	5 7 C. R. 8 H.
ETRICOURT	10	-	Resting.	"
"	11	-	Battalion moved to HINDENBURG Line near RIBECOURT.	"
RIBECOURT	12	-	Battalion moved to line in the evening in relief of 1st Leicester Regt – K.O.C. in Front Line – D Company in support.	57.c K 30. 57.c L.20 and L.21
"	13	-	Battalion remained in Line 12/13 rather night of 15/1/17 – during day in trenches	
"	14	-	enemy artillery fairly quiet – at intervals during day and night enemy artillery shelled RIBECOURT Sun artillery carried out usual barrages on enemy back areas.	
"	15	-	2 Other wounded on 15. 2 Other wounded 16th. Other company relief night	"
"	16	-	of 15/1/17. Battalion relieved by 1 East Lancs Regt, D'Ade night of 15/17 and	
"	17	-	proceeded to dugouts in Brigade Reserve.	
"	18			

WAR DIARY
or
INTELLIGENCE SUMMARY.

(Erase heading not required.)

Army Form C. 2118.

Instructions regarding War Diaries and Intelligence Summaries are contained in F. S. Regs., Part II. and the Staff Manual respectively. Title pages will be prepared in manuscript.

Place	Date 1917 Dec	Hour	Summary of Events and Information	Remarks and references to Appendices
Mt RIBECOURT	19	—	In Brigade Reserve — Enemy artillery active at intervals during the day. Shelling RIBECOURT + pt	57C.
"	20	—	Working parties. 2 Other ranks wounded on 20.1 sentries.	ditto
"	21	—	8 Glouster Regiment and proceeded to Camps in HAVRINCOURT WOOD. Battalion relieved night of 22/23rd by	ditto
HAVRINCOURT WOOD	22	'	Resting.	ditto
"	23	'	Resting.	ditto
"	24	—	Resting — Battalion spiked Enemies Gas Balloons.	ditto
Nr. RIBECOURT	25	—	Battalion moved to HINDENBURG Line on relief of 9 Cheshire Regt.	57C P122.
"	26		Working party of 70 men found	ditto
"	27		do	ditto
"	28		Moved to support subsector of left sector of Divisional Frontier relief of the 7th E/Lanes. Battn. HQ L.20.d.05.90.	ditto
"	29		2 other ranks wounded. Enemy activity normal during the day — much firing by night.	ditto
"	30		Barrage by enemy well away on right flank at 6.30am lasting until about 7.30am. Only a few shells on Battn Area	ditto
"	31.		Normal.	ditto

A.A. Ryan Lt.Col.
C. Weller R.

58/19

WA 31

Confidential

War Diary

of

6(S) Bn Wiltshire Regt-

From 1st to 31 Jany 1918

Volume 31.

Army Form C. 2118.

WAR DIARY
or
INTELLIGENCE SUMMARY.
(Erase heading not required.)

Instructions regarding War Diaries and Intelligence Summaries are contained in F. S. Regs., Part II. and the Staff Manual respectively. Title pages will be prepared in manuscript.

Place	Date	Hour	Summary of Events and Information	Remarks and references to Appendices
	July 1918			
	1st		Very quiet day – Patrols sent out.	
	2nd		Quiet day – Patrols sent out.	
	3rd		Battalion relieved by Irish Regt and moved to support line in cellars of RIQCOURT & NINE WOOD	
RIQCOURT	4th		Battalion resting and cleaning up.	
	5		Battalion relieved by 22nd London Regiment and proceeded to HINDENBURG Line.	
HINDENBURG LINE	6th		Battalion relieved 10th Hussars Regt in support – centre sub-sector Kabul Road & Kabul Avenue	
"	7		Quiet day – Working parties	
"	8		Quiet day – Working parties	
"	9		Lt. H.S. Rogers wounded. 1 Other rank killed. – Relieved 9 Cheshire Regt in centre	
IN THE TRENCHES	10		Subsector. A, C & D Coys in front line. B Co in Support Gouzet present	
"	11		1 Other rank killed – Very quiet day	
"	12		Lieut A.G. Orwin wounded but remained on duty – 7 Other ranks wounded.	
"	13		Quiet day.	
			Lt Co. Company killed. D relieving C Coy. B relieving A Coy. C relieving B Coy and D relieving A Coy. B Coy patrols attacked to Battalion Left line.	
	14		Enemy artillery at intervals during day shelled vicinity of HQ & Howitzers.	

WAR DIARY
or
INTELLIGENCE SUMMARY.
(Erase heading not required.)

Army Form C. 2118.

Instructions regarding War Diaries and Intelligence Summaries are contained in F. S. Regs., Part II. and the Staff Manual respectively. Title pages will be prepared in manuscript.

Place	Date	Hour	Summary of Events and Information	Remarks and references to Appendices
	1916 Jan.y			
IN THE LINE	15		Battalion relieved by Welch Regt moving transport in VALLEY Trench. "C" Company remaining in line attached to 9th A.L.I.B.	
VALLEY TRENCH	16		Relieved by 7 S. Lancs Regt and marched to DRANE Camp.	aly 57 c
DRANE CAMP	17		Battalion resting and cleaning up.	aly P 186
"	18		Usual Company inspection. Baths	aly
"	19		Strength 7 12 other ranks joined	aly
"	20		Sunday. Church Parade. Working parties.	aly
"	21		Morning Inspection	
"	21/22		Received 10 Worcester Regt on night bombers "B" and "D" Coys in Front Line - "D"	2/A McSWERIE
"			on Left. on Right. "C" in Reserve.	aly
MT PREMIER	22		Enemy artillery active. Shelling our outpost line - 5 other Ranks Killed.	aly
"			"A" in Company relief "D" relieving "B" Coy. "C" Coy relieving "D" Coy	aly
"	23		1 other Rank killed + 2 wounded. - Enemy at intervals during the day Shelling	aly
"			in vicinity of Headquarters. "A" Company relief "B" Coy relieving "A" Coy. "B" Coy	aly
"			relieving "C" Coy.	aly
"	24		3 other ranks wounded one + other ranks killed. "A" Company relief "D" Coy relieving "B"	aly
			"C" Coy relieving A Coy.	

Army Form C. 2118.

WAR DIARY
or
INTELLIGENCE SUMMARY.
(Erase heading not required.)

Instructions regarding War Diaries and Intelligence Summaries are contained in F. S. Regs., Part II. and the Staff Manual respectively. Title pages will be prepared in manuscript.

Place	Date	Hour	Summary of Events and Information	Remarks and references to Appendices
HANES CAMP	Jany 1918 25		Battalion relieved by 10 Worcester Regt and proceeded to HANES CAMP	57 C.
"	26.		Resting and cleaning up.	P.18 F.
"	27		Sunday. Church Parade	
"	28		Usual Company Inspection, cleaning up, baths	
"	29		Battalion relieved 10 Worcester Regt in right subsector. A & B in frontline	
"	30		D Coy in support. C Coy in reserve. 2/Lt Coffey mortally wounded. Died at 9th Ambulance	
"	31		Quiet day in front line. Enemy shelling using timber	
			Slight bombardment evening. Stand to on the way to trenches producing gas shells otherwise Quiet day – D Coy Supplied with B Coy prior to stand to	

J.P. Lyman Major
Comdg 6/Wiltshire Regt.

Confidential

War Diary
of
6(S) 8th Wiltshire Regt.

Volume 32

From 1st to 28 Feb 1918.

WAR DIARY or INTELLIGENCE SUMMARY.

(Erase heading not required.)

Army Form C. 2118.

Instructions regarding War Diaries and Intelligence Summaries are contained in F. S. Regs., Part II. and the Staff Manual respectively. Title pages will be prepared in manuscript.

Place	Date 1918	Hour	Summary of Events and Information	Remarks and references to Appendices
IN THE LINE	1 Aug		Battalion relieved by 9th Royal West Surreys, and proceeded by train to SERZING Camp.	57C
VALLULART CAMP	2		Battalion moved to VALLULART WOOD Camp.	P.28 a
"	3		Bath, resting and generally cleaning up.	"
"	4		Station warning - Arms drill &c.	"
"	5		Platoon training.	"
"	6		Battalion proceeded by train to ROSCAULT, & leaving S. Rancastel on NINE WOOD
IN THE LINE	7		B Company (Right Front), D Company (Left Front), C Company (Left Support). A by Right Support. Relieved at 2200 night 7/8th.	at NINE WOOD
"			Night Support, Party shelling of TRESCAULT RIBECOURT Road. Nil casualties received. Enemy artillery quiet during day - much machine gun fire at night.	"
"	8		Quiet day.	"
"	9		Quiet day. 1 Other rank killed - 1 wounded.	"
"	10		Battalion relieved by Gordons and proceeded to the Beaucamp Line.	"
"	11		Working party for front line at night.	"
"	12		Quiet day.	"
"	13		Quiet day. Battalion relieved by 4th Bedfordshire Regiment and proceeded to VALLULART Camp by train - arriving in Camp at 5/15 am 14/8/18.	"
M ROCQUIGNY	14		Battalion moved to Camp N. ROCQUIGNY -	57C
"	15		Platoon training.	O.33A
"	16		Platoon training. Arms drill &c.	"
"	17		Church Parade.	"
"	18		Platoon training - Arms drill at Bngt of the Other Ranks forward.	"

Army Form C. 2118.

WAR DIARY
or
INTELLIGENCE SUMMARY.
(Erase heading not required.)

Instructions regarding War Diaries and Intelligence Summaries are contained in F. S. Regs., Part II. and the Staff Manual respectively. Title pages will be prepared in manuscript.

Place	Date	Hour	Summary of Events and Information	Remarks and references to Appendices
M. ROCQUIGNY	19 20 21 22		Eaton Company training. Musketry - firing on range.	
	23		Brigade Tactical Scheme carried out night of 23/7/17. Battalion moved to camp near HAPLINCOURT. Barclay Coy.	
HAPLINCOURT	24 25 26		[illegible] Coy [illegible] [illegible] D Coy range Company training - Musketry and Bayonet Fighting	57C OAD
"	27		B, C + D Companies proceeded to forward area for work in forward area. A Company H Company remaining in Camp. At 8/30pm orders received that Battalion would occupy third system of defence, which was carried out.	
"	28		Company training - NCOs class under L. Greenwood.	

A.J. Hughes
Lt Col
Loyal North Lancashire Regiment

19th Division.
58th Infantry Brigade.

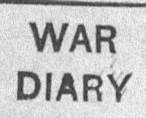

6th BATTALION

WILTSHIRE REGIMENT

MARCH 1 9 1 8

Narrative of Operations attached.
Lessons learnt from the operations.

Confidential.

War Diary

of

6(S) B⁺ Wiltshire Regiment.

From 1ˢᵗ to 31ˢᵗ March 1918

Volume 33.

Vol 33

Army Form C. 2118.

WAR DIARY
or
INTELLIGENCE SUMMARY.
(Erase heading not required.)

Instructions regarding War Diaries and Intelligence Summaries are contained in F. S. Regs., Part II. and the Staff Manual respectively. Title pages will be prepared in manuscript.

I

Place	Date	Hour	Summary of Events and Information	Remarks and references to Appendices
SANDERS CAMP.	1918 Feb. 1		Company & Platoon Training & Musketry on range.	a.b. 57c
	2		Company & Platoon Training & Musketry on range.	a.b. O & d.
	3		Church Parade and 15 Platoon won the Brigade A.R.A. Competition.	a.b.
	4		Company & Platoon Training and Musketry on range.	a.b.
	5		Found Working Party of 300 O.Rs. for work on the Third System also a Working Party of 20 O.Rs. erecting huts at BAPAUME.	a.b.
	6		Company & Platoon Training & Musketry on range.	a.b.
	7		Company & Platoon Training & Musketry on range. Reconnaissance by Officers & NCOs of Counter Attack Scheme.	a.b.
	8		Battalion took part in Brigade practice move to DOIGNIES Counter Attack Assembly Position and Deployment to advance Assembly Positions Third System.	a.b. a.b. a.b.
	9		Church Parade and Reconnaissance by Officers and NCOs of Second and Third System.	a.b.
	10		Company & Platoon Training and Musketry on range. Reconnaissance by Officers and NCOs of Second & Third System.	a.b.
	11		Battalion Working Party working on Third System.	a.b.
HAPLINCOURT	12		Company and Platoon Training and Musketry on range. Reconnaissance by Officers and NCOs of Second & Third System.	a.b.
	13		Battalion Working Party working on Third System.	a.b.
	14		Brigade Scheme (WRTS & RWF) with an Enemy & RWF as attacking troops.	a.b.
	15		Church Parade.	a.b.
	16		Battalion Working Party, working on Third System.	a.b.
	17		Battalion Scheme. Practice Assembly and deployment to Advanced Assembly Position.	a.b.

WAR DIARY or INTELLIGENCE SUMMARY

Army Form C. 2118.

Place	Date	Hour	Summary of Events and Information	Remarks and references to Appendices
SANDERS Camp	1918 March 20 2/R. 28th		Brigade Scheme (WILTS & RWF) with "Tanks". RWF as Enemy & Wilts assaulting troops. Battalion took part in active operations on German offensive including battles for MORCHIES, BEUGNY, FREMICOURT, BAPAUME, GREVILLERS, YPRES, HEBUTERNE.	
	21		Intense bombardment in early morning. Battalion ordered to Stand by at 5.23 a.m. Moved to Assembly Position GAIKA Copse 11.30am. Moved to Deployment position for counter attack on DOIGNIES at 4.30am consolidating position in support of 57 Brigade. Battalion moved up 21 Officers & 475 O/Ranks.	
	22		Moved to ground W. of LEBUCQUIRE at 2.30am. Moved to MORCHIES at 11.30am and consolidated 3rd line of Defence from MORCHIES village to Sugar factory on BAPAUME Road. 'D' 'A' & 'C' Companies in front, 'B' Coy. in our Support, Battalion HQ. in SUNKEN Road immediately in rear of 'B' Coy. At 4.45pm Enemy advanced from N. & N.E. checked by our Shell, Lewis Gun and Rifle fire on line LAGNICOURT – VAULX. Heavy casualties inflicted on the enemy. Counter attack by tanks on our left threw the enemy back.	
	23		During night 22/23rd troops in front of us fell back to our line which now became the line of resistance. Troops on our right flank S. of BAPAUME Road fell back leaving our right flank unprotected. Defensive flank formed on our right. General attack on all positions by enemy started at 8am. All frontal advances by enemy were repulsed by steady & controlled rifle & Lewis gun fire. At 2.15 pm order received from Bde. to fall back. Owing to general attack being in progress and the nature of the ground — a glacis upward slope — heavily barraged and swept by cross fire from enemy machine guns — it was decided to try to hold on until	

WAR DIARY
or
INTELLIGENCE SUMMARY.

Army Form C. 2118.

Place	Date 1918 March	Hour	Summary of Events and Information	Remarks and references to Appendices
	23 (cont)		nightfall and slow withdraw. It was not known until later that troops on our right had fallen back to such an extent as to give no covering fire to our left flank. At 4 p.m. enemy entirely checked by the steadiness of our men. Upon an enveloping movement on our right and left flanks. As we were being outflanked, orders were issued to withdraw to next system of defence behind BEUGNY at 5 p.m. Battalion withdrew by a rearguard action. Many men sacrificing their lives in covering the withdrawal of their comrades. Enemy placed heavy artillery barrage on our line of withdrawal and swept our retirement with machine cross-fire from his machine guns behind our position. On reforming 6 officers (2 of whom wounded) and 32 men were present. The transport and Surplus Personnel moved from SANDERS Camp, HAPLINCOURT at 10 a.m. via BANCOURT arriving at 11 a.m. and leaving 1 hour later, parking in a field S.E. of BAPAUME. Reinforcement of 81 O. Ranks left at 7 p.m. to join remnants of Battalion holding the line.	
	24		Rearguard action fought through FREMICOURT – BAPAUME to line GREVILLERS – THILLOY where the Division consolidated a system of defence on dirch. 5th Brigade with its right on BAPAUME Road G.11.c.15. on left of Brigade with 37 Brigade on its left. Transport and Personnel moved to outskirts of GREVILLERS, thence to IRLES stopping en-route until 6 p.m.	25th
	25		Enemy opened attack at 6 a.m., adopting at once outflanking movements on our right flank. He was entirely held for some hours and attempted a frontal attack. At 11:30 a.m. throwing in new troops he worked round our right flank and our sucksses by a reargns a flanking action suffering heavily at this time from shell fire, (including gas shells + rifle grenade and cross fire from machine guns. At 1 p.m. withdrawal to trenches etc.	

WAR DIARY
INTELLIGENCE SUMMARY

Army Form C. 2118.

(Erase heading not required.)

Instructions regarding War Diaries and Intelligence Summaries are contained in F. S. Regs., Part II. and the Staff Manual respectively. Title pages will be prepared in manuscript.

Place	Date	Hour	Summary of Events and Information	Remarks and references to Appendices
	1918 March 26 (cont)		W. of LOUPART Wood where a stand was made. Troops on our right continued to fall back and a further withdrawal to a defensive position E. of IRLES was made. Troops on our right flank had now completely given way and after fighting a delaying action at this point, a further withdrawal was made through MIRAUMONT where an outpost line was established to E. of PUISSIEUX where an outpost line was established. 3 Battalions of the Brigade being formed into a composite Battalion. Transport moved from IRLES to ACHIET-LE-PETIT arriving Q ?? again at 12 noon to BUCQUOY and at 3/30 p.m. to PUISSIEUX. Marched night 25/26 from PUISSIEUX to SOUASTRE via COURCAMP arriving at 2 a.m.	A.G. A.G. A.G.
	26th & 27th		During night 25/26 13th Composite Battalion (being very weak in numbers) were relieved and withdrew forming successive lines of outposts about HEBUTERNE - FONQUEVILLERS - and in front of BAYENCOURT where battalions were re-inforced and a strong line of outposts established forming the the 3rd line of Defence. Enemy held along the line BEAUMONT HAMEL - SERRE.	A.G.
	28		Bde. Composite Battalion relieved by a Canadian Battalion and Battalion moved to FAMECHON after inspection and congratulation by G.O.C. Division. Casualties were as follows - 2/Lt C. GREENWOOD Killed in Action; Lt. E.E. PEGGE Wounded & Missing; Lieut. J. STOGDON Wounded & Missing; Lieut. S.H. WILLIAMS Wounded & Missing; 2/Lieut. D.B. CAMPBELL Wounded & Missing; 2/Lt L.R. MILLERSHIP Wounded & Missing; 2/Lt B. AUGUSTIN Wounded & Missing; Lt. M.G. SUMNER Wounded & Missing; Capt. F.H. BONE Wounded; Lt. W. G. PRICE Wounded; Lt. Col. Lord A.G. THYNNE D.S.O. Wounded; Lt. F.J. OXLEY Wounded; 2/Lt. C.R. FRIEND Wounded; 2/Lt. M. SILLARS Wounded; 2/Lt. L.E. EDWARDS Wounded; 2/Lt. G. SNOOK Wounded;	A.G.

Army Form C. 2118.

WAR DIARY
or
INTELLIGENCE SUMMARY.
(Erase heading not required.)

Place	Date 1918 March	Hour	Summary of Events and Information	Remarks and references to Appendices
	29/30.		2/Lt. G. Smith Wounded; Major C.S. Audry Missing; Capt. N.L. Flower Missing, Capt Goodwick R.A.M.C. M.O., Missing; Capt. R. Garthwaite M.C. Wounded (Remained at Duty) Other Ranks 497 (Killed, Wounded & Missing). Left Famechon at 9.15pm and marched to Candas arriving at 6 a.m. Entrained at Candas at 3.30 p.m. Moved by Lorries to Birr Barracks Locre arriving at 6 p.m.	
	31		Army Commander inspected NCOs and men who took part in active operations at 12.45pm. Reorganising Battalion.	
			The above is the skeleton summary of the work performed by the 6 (S) Wilts Regt. during the month of March. It is respectfully submitted, however, that the simulation embodied by the form of the official summary fail to do justice to the effort made by the Battalion and to the results achieved. The stand made by the Battalion at Morchies from 4 a.m on the 22nd March to 5 pm on the 23rd and all that it meant, is a glorious episode in the history of the Wiltshire Regiment. It is a heroic record of self sacrifice stemming the victorious rush of a superior enemy and a model lesson of a rearguard fight. The subsequent retirement from Fremicourt through Bapaume to Grevillers and thence to Bayencourt was only one endless and stubborn fight. Suffice it to say that only one officer, 1 Sergeant, and 15 Other Ranks came out the struggle, and those officers have also been commingled.	

Narrative of Operations 21-29 March 1918 (1)
2 WILTSHIRE REGT.

21st 5.23 a.m. Order from Bde. to "STAND BY"
    11.30 a.m.   "   "   Move to ASSEMBLY positions
    12.25 "   Arrived at assembly position GAIKA COPSE
    4.30 p.m. Moved to Deployment position for DOIGNIES counter
               attack scheme – Dug in in Support 57 Bde.

22nd 2.15   Orders recd. to Move to ground W of LEBUCQUIERE
            Bn. moved later to MILL – Cross Roads
            halting there for remainder of night.

     11 am Move to positions about MORCHIES 4th Corps front
            Line of posts dug in East of sunken road
            MORCHIES – SUGAR BEET FACTORY on
            BAPAUME – CAMBRAI Rd
            D.A.C. Coys from left to Right. B Co in Support

            Troops in front 1 Coy 57th Bde (about 60 men)
            dug in in posts about 250x in front
            Pt of Bn. 10th Cheshire (25 Div) about 1000x
            in front on Sunken road MORCHIES – CRUCIFIX
            on Bapaume Rd. remainder of 10th Cheshire
            in MORCHIES village.

            Troops on left of R.W.F. our left being
            swung back to connect with them.

            Troops on right 56th Bde on S. of Bapaume Rd.
            up to night 22/23.

     4 pm. Attack Enemy moved to attack on our
            positions from line LARNICOURT – VAULX
            advance coming from N E direction

(2)

22nd — Troops holding line MORCHIES – CRUCIFIX began to fall back on our positions.

Enemy advance continued – no frontal attack on our positions facing E. being attempted. Our Lewis guns & riflemen opened fire at 1200* to our front on all troops moving across our front in S.W direction.

Small parties of enemy continued to move across our front at long range to low ground & valley near Sunken road MORCHIES – CRUCIFIX line.

5pm — Counter Attack by Tanks made on our left. Enemy thrown back and further advance checked for day.

8pm — Our post nearest MORCHIES raided by enemy patrol from village. Raid repulsed, enemy leaving 1 killed.

Quiet during remainder of night.

23rd — Patrols sent out in early morning to try to get touch with troops in front of us or on our right – & reported that

(i) Enemy occupied MORCHIES – CRUCIFIX line

(ii) Our right flank was not in touch with 56 Bde – & no troops were on our immediate right.

(* this report not received until about 1300)

(3)

<u>23d</u> At 8a.m. Enemy advance continued from N & N.E. & enemy troops in small parties moved across our front towards Bapaume Road at 1300x range. No frontal attack attempted by enemy at this time. Heavy shelling on Bn. H.Q. sunken road in 17a & our front lines, by heavy guns which were firing over our heads from N.W. direction & appeared to be our own guns.

Enemy shell fire now increased & machine gun fire swept all slopes between MORCHIES & BEUGNY making movement difficult.

1pm. In order to protect our flank & rear a Coy of 10 Cheshire was placed facing Bapaume Road — this was supplemented by 2 platoons from our Support Coy.

2pm. General attack by enemy on all our positions.
Order to ~~retire~~ withdraw received from Bde at 2.15pm owing to nature of ground behind us — a glacis slope up to BEUGNY & the fact that an attack on all our positions was in progress it was considered impossible to withdraw & it was decided to hold on until nightfall

23rd It was not at that time fully realized that we were left entirely unprotected from our right rear. It was also hoped that by holding on until nightfall & keeping Enemy in check at this point the defence of the next line of resistence might be organized & consolidated.

4pm. Enemy began to get round our position. Flanks on right from SUGAR FACTORY & on left from MORCHIES. They were however held in check by the steadiness of our troops who refused to give way & kept up a steady & well directed fire on all approaches. A stubborn resistence was made and heavy casualties were inflicted on the Enemy whenever they attempted to advance.

At 4.30pm a general enveloping movement by the Enemy, who had collected considerable forces S. of Bapaume Rd, made withdrawal necessary. Orders to do so issued accordingly.

At 5pm. Batt? withdrew under heavy barrage & heavy cross fire from Enemy machine guns to blue line East of FREMICOURT, where reorganization took place.

(5)

22nd 6pm 6 officers (2 of whom were wounded) and 32 men were present when Bn. was reformed. Later supplemented by a draft of 64 new men from Depot

23/24 Intermittent shelling & continual m/g fire on our positions during night. shelling increasing towards daylight

24th Heavy shelling & machine gun fire in which we lost another officer & several men. Subsequent withdrawal to lines about Bapaume

24/25th Withdrawal to line GREVILLERS – THILLOY where Division was reformed.
56th Bde on right of Bapaume Road with one Bn. in Div. Support.
58th Bde with its right resting on Bapaume Rd
57th " with its left on GREVILLERS
our forces being disposed in depth.
6th Wiltshire 3 lines of 3 posts each – 8 men to a post – at intervals of 100x & distances of 150x

25th Battle of GREVILLERS.
8am. Strong attacks supported by M.G. fire on our right flank along Bapaume Rd. necessitating our rear 2 lines of posts being

(6)

being moved across to reinforce right flank along Bapaume Rd.

No frontal attack from Enemy attempted.

Enemy adopted outflanking tactics entirely & at 11 a.m. we commenced rearguard & flank guard action. Our front posts covering retirement by steady Lewis gun & rifle fire supplemented by machine guns.

All our positions heavily shelled & rifle grenaded at the time. Enemy employing gas shells. We also came under fire from our own field guns. Organized retirement was difficult.

1 pm. Withdrawal to system of trenches on high ground west of GREVILLERS where we continued. Suffered heavily from shell & m/g fire from enemy from ridges to S. of Bapaume Rd.

This system of trenches was an unfavourable position owing to dead ground along country around it of which the enemy took full advantage in assembling his troops, and eventually

2 pm. troops withdrew to W. & N.W. of LOUPART WOOD.

S.A.A. at the time was short.

An excellent opportunity now occurred for making a good stand as we could hold all approaches to this position but owing to action of troops on right of 19th Division on relieving

(7)

25th towards IRLES practically in mass the opportunity was lost.

A good stand was made by part of 19 Div: NW of LOUPART Wood (chiefly Royal Warwicks) held up enemy advance for about 40 minutes Steady & controlled fire by these troops on Edge of wood help enemy entirely in check and had their flanks been supported a position might have been consolidated here — as it was the enemy advance was delayed by this resolute stand and the retiring troops were enabled to withdraw in safety.

Eventually the enemy at this point by means of a fold in the ground were able to creep round & assemble for an assault on the position and these troops withdrew in an orderly rearguard action after inflicting heavy casualties on enemy & suffering very slightly themselves. At 3.15 pm.
Three aeroplanes assisted withdrawal by harassing fire.

A further stand was made in trenches in front of IRLES by our troops (19th Div.)

There was a subsequent withdrawal through MIRAUMONT to ground E of PUISIEUX where a line of outposts was established

25/26 Our troops finally withdrew to line of outposts at HEBUTERNE.

26th & 57th — Successive lines of outposts established at HEBUTERNE — FONQUILLERS & BAYENCOURT.

28th — Brigade withdrew via COIGNEUX to FAMECHON.

2/4/18

Alan Cun Howatt
Captain
6 Wiltshire Regt

(1)

Ask Director of the
regime anything further
with regard to Session."
ags.

File there — I shall
probably want them
again in any case.

(I)   ...ority for pushing   units in
                       ... to deal with   support in
                       ...while they which
                       ...as well in advance
                       ...infantry.   withdrawal
                       ...ing-fire and fire-
                       ...guard actions. This
                       ...sighting of rifles,
(II)   ...ition in addition   could
                       ...meaning of the terms.   of the Enemy
                       ...wasted, and rifles
                       ...sighted.   ting fire

                       ...nce into "blobs"
(III)   ...a withdrawal. This   ls were
                       ...treated on the 24th   wce and
                       ...my shelled intensely   ties.
                       ...had to be passed
                       ...w casualties were   frontal fire

                       ...acquiring the idea
(III)   ...is necessary if the   ontal attack
                                                  improvement
                       d Williams
                       Major
                       9th Welsh Regt

(IV) That the moving up ...us of small lights
thrown up by first waves of infantry had an
effective & rapid means of informing his
artillery at what positions he was held
in check.

(1)

— Lessons learnt —

(1) The urgent necessity for pushing forward Lewis Guns to deal with the advanced hostile M.Gs which work from positions well in advance of the leading infantry.

(2) The value of covering-fire and fire control in rear-guard actions. This means accurate sighting of rifles, economy of ammunition in addition to the ordinary meaning of the terms. Ammunition was wasted, and rifles were rarely correctly sighted.

(3) The collecting of men into "blobs" in the course of a withdrawal. This was clearly demonstrated on the 24th March when the enemy shelled intensely the ground which had to be passed over, and very few casualties were sustained.

(4) The grave danger of acquiring the idea that a withdrawal is necessary if the flanks fall away.

10²/- 2/4/18.

H Lloyd Williams
Maj'r.
9th Welch Regt

(1) ... units in support in

(II) ... withdrawal

... could ... the Enemy ... ting fire ... to were ... ure and ... ties ... frontal fire ... ... tal attack ... concealment

(IV) That the Enemy by means of small lights thrown up by first waves of infantry had an effective & rapid means of informing his artillery at what points he was held in check.

Operations 21/28 March 1918

(I.) That close communication between posts & units is unnecessary if cooperation & mutual support is established.
Failure breaking this, caused premature withdrawal from good positions.

(II) That small determined bodies of troops could always hold up superior numbers of the enemy if their flanks are covered by supporting fire.

(III) Even if not so covered resolute stands were always successful in checking advance and compelling enemy to alter his tactics.
Enemy never faced steady & controlled frontal fire in their advance.

(II) That the enemy seldom pushed a frontal attack, always relying on a flanking movement to turn us out of our position.

(IV) That the enemy by means of small lights thrown up by forward waves of infantry had an effective & rapid means of informing his artillery at what positions he was held in check.

(2)

(V) That enemy machine guns were well to the front at each advance and were rapidly in position at each check and materially assisted his advance especially when a cross fire was opened on our positions.

(VI) That the majority of our troops did not understand rearguard & delaying actions and during the early stages of the retirement troops withdrew in bunches, no covering fire being brought to bear and no delaying action fought.

(VII) That the general tendency was to withdraw to high ground which rapidly came under shell fire and long range machine gun fire; the valleys were often ignored allowing enemy to make use of dead ground.

(VIII) That there was a useless waste of S.A.A. & Lewis guns rifle at long ranges resulting in a serious shortage when enemy came under short effective ranges.

(ix) That in a general retirement it is absolutely necessary for ~~Brigade~~ Staff Officers (if possible mounted) to be present at the successive lines of resistance to control +direct the withdrawal & delaying actions of large masses of infantry which the various units of which inevitably become mixed.

Alan Gartwaite
Captain 6th Wiltshire Regt

2.4.18

3

(IX) That in a general retirement it is absolutely necessary for a certain № Staff Officers (if possible mounted) to be present at the + directly successive lines of resistance, to control the withdrawal & delay which has become t[...]

2.4.18

Notes from Major MONTREAL

Dear Garthwaite,

To my mind the tactical lessons of the stunt are:—

1. That no number of lines of trenches is impregnable against a superior enemy determined to pay the price of capturing.

2. That the defensive value of obstacles has been materially discounted by the latest weapons of demolition.

3. That defensive infantry unsupported by artillery and aircraft is paralysed in the face of the combined aircraft, artillery, and infantry of the enemy.

4. That machine guns in trenches are doomed to destruction by hostile artillery where the latter has established a superiority over the opposing artillery.

5. That everything considered, the instruction of the Offrs. N.C.O. and men in Open Warfare has again become an essential part of their training.

58th Brigade.
19th Division.

WAR DIARY NOT RECEIVED BY HISTORICAL SECTION

NARRATIVE OF EVENTS

1/6th BATTALION WILTSHIRE REGIMENT

APRIL 1918.

H.Q. 58th Inf.Bde.

April 1918.

Herewith Narrative of Events from 10th April - 20th April during operations near WYTSCHAETE.

H.W.HOUSE,

Major,
6th Wilts. Regt.,

April 25 1918.

6th Wiltshire Yeomanry Battn.
The Wiltshire Regt.

Narrative of events during the operations from April 10th - April 20th 1918.

On the night of the 9th/10th April the Battn. was holding a subsector of the trenches east of the MESSINES-WYTSCHAETE ridge - with its right on the WAMBEKE & its left on JUNCTION BUILDINGS (exclusive). The front was held by two Coys. (A & B) which were distributed in depth - each with two platoons in the front line of posts & 1 strong platoon in support. C & D Coys. were in reserve about 2000 yds. behind the front line.
About 3.30 a.m. fairly heavy shelling on the whole subsector began consisting of H.E. & gas shells. This continued practically without intermission the whole though no gas shells fell after about 5.30 a.m.
About 6 a.m. the shelling which was much heavier on the subsector of the Battalions on our right reached a climax, and the enemy under cover of a very thick "scotch mist" attacked the 57th Bde. on the right & apparently forced its centre Battn. back on to its reserve line. The left Bn. of the 57th Bde. (the 10th Warwick R.) thereby had its right flank turned & the success of the attack was so sudden that a portion of the Warwicks were forced to fall back in a northerly direction on to our right flank - the WAMBEKE formed the natural boundary between the 57th & 58th Bdes. - & just North of it ran a long duck-boarded but shallow Communication trench, MANCHESTER ST. Between VERNE RD. & GUN farm was a system of flooded shallow trenches, which "C" Coy. occupied at once to form a defensive position, while half the support platoon of B Coy. was utilized with any parties of the 10th WARWICK R. which came across the BEKE to man MANCHESTER ST. as a long defensive flank.
The 4th Coy. (D Coy) was used to stiffen up the defence of the right flank of the Bde. which was so dangerously exposed.
The whole Bn. subsector was subjected to heavy shelling and a large part of it to M.G. & rifle fire throughout the day, the M.G. & rifle fire coming from the high ground South of WAMBEKE round ANZAC FARM.
The Bn. maintained its position everywhere until 4.30 p.m. that afternoon. At 3.30 p.m. the enemy was massing 2000 yds. east of our front line - & a frontal attack developed, but was unable to materialise owing to our vigorous Lewis & gun & rifle fire.
At 4.30 p.m. orders were received by the Battn. on our left (9th R.W.F.) to evacuate the front line of posts; & as this order emanated from Bde. the front line held by this Bn. was also abandoned, although the order for this to be done never reached the front line from our Bn.H.Q. A strong position was then taken up by the two front Coys. on the line of the supporting points. The enemy advanced about 5.30 p.m. to our original front line, but was unable to approach nearer than 600 or 800 yds. owing to our active Lewis gun & rifle fire.
About 6 p.m. the enemy organised strong attacks on our right & left flanks - The order to withdraw on to the Reserve Line never reached the front line Coys. so our positions on the support line were held until the enemy

had completely surrounded the two front line Coy. a few elements of which, only, managed to work through to our own lines.

The reserve Coys. which had been heavily engaged on the right flank, fell back fighting on to the high ground WEST of OOSTAVERNE. Battn. H.Q. Coy. which was utilised in an attempt to strengthen the right rear was also engaged heavily in fighting in which the C.O. Major Monreal was mortally wounded & the 2nd in Command Capt. Garthwaite wounded.

During the night the survivors of the Battn. rallied on portions of the front ~~railhead~~ between the DAMMSTRASSE & WYTSCHAETE. 75 stragglers were collected & sent up to GRAND BOIS, where Capt. Rentoul had established Bn.H.Q. The remainder of the day was spent in collecting & re-organising the Battn.

On the 12th April the Bn. was withdrawn to ROSSIGNOL CAMP, near KEMMEL.

270 Reinforcements were waiting here & the Battn. was re-organised mustering 450 strong - and moved to BABADOS camp via CLYTTE for the night.

13th April

At 10.30 a.m. <u>the next day</u> orders were received to stand by ready to move & a quarter of an hour later the Battn. was ordered to march to a position of readiness between LA CLYTTE & KEMMEL east of the main road. At 12 noon C.Os. were warned that the Bde. would take over the line that night from the S.African Bde. Details of the relief could not be given till 4.30 pm. at the S.African Bde. H.Q. & then were very complicated. The Bn. was to take over from 4 units - a portion of the 4th S.African Bn. the whole of the 1st S.African Bn. 2 Coys. of the 10th R.Warwick R. & 1 Coy. of the S.W.B. The front of it was to take over was about 800 yds. & included the extremely important high ground at the SPANBROEK - MOLEN CRATER.

The Bn. marched up from its position of readiness and although ~~eventually~~ all companies were in position by 3 a.m. the relief was not reported complete till 6 a.m.

The Bn. was disposed as follows from left to right -
A Coy. two platoons, front line One support east of SPANBROEK MOLEN CRATER.

<u>B. C. & D Coys.</u> each two platoons in the front line & one in support, from left to right.

On the right of D Coy. were the 12th R.I.R. and on the left of A Coy. were the 9th R.W.F.

Bn. H.Q. were 300 yards in rear of the front line just W. of SPANBROEK MOLEN CRATER.

The 14th April was an abnormally quiet day; the enemy Artillery was more or less inactive except on the area round Bn.H.Q. which ~~eventually~~ later moved to REGENT ST. DUG OUTS. N.29.c.central.

On the night of the 14th it was decided that the dispositions of the Bn. required adjustment - It was decided to push up the whole of A & D Coys into the front line & withdraw the whole of B & C Coys. into support, B on the left C on the right, covering A & D respectively.

In addition to ensure the security of SPANBROEK MOLEN the G.O.C. placed 1 Coy. of the 9th Welch at the disposal of O.C. 6th Wilts R. The O.C. this Coy. (B Coy) was accordingly ordered to send 1 platoon to be in close support to A Coy. just East of the CRATER, and place the remainder of his Company in a position S.West of the CRATER from which it would be ready to launch an immediate counter attack against the high ground should this be lost, or reinforce the front lines.

These alterations in the dispositions of the Battn. were carried out during the night of the 14th/15th.

At dawn on the 15th the enemy opened a heavy H.E. barrage on the whole subsector particularly along the support line, and in the area round REGENT ST DUG OUTS.
About 5.45 a.m. the S.O.S. went up on the left Coy. front. The enemy were attacking on the right Coy. front, and on the front of the Battn. on our right.
The attack failed to reach our front line, but the enemy succeeded in penetrating the front of the 12th R.I.R. who were at the time attempting to carry out a withdrawal, using their left flank as a pivot - The enemy occupied R.E. & SHELL FARMS and made it necessary, first for half of C Coy. to move up & occupy a line, running approximately E. & W. North of SHELL farm and secondly for D Coy. in order to safeguard its right flank, to bend its right back on to the left of the C Coy's front line.
The line therefore was intact, though thinly held; enemy snipers and machine guns were extremely active, & being close, hindered the movement & the organisation of our new front on the Southern flank.
On the remainder of the Battn. front enemy movement was vigorously checked by snipers & lewis guns - In spite of very heavy shelling in the earlier part of the day, casualties on the left half of the front were slight.
As the line was so thinly held on the right, it was decided to dribble 1 platoon of B Coy. of the 9th Welch up into the front line held by C & D Coys. and to move 1 platoon up into support behind D Coy's left. This was successfully done.
That night orders were received to withdraw from the front line South of the SPANBROEK MOLEN CRATER - This meant that the line occupied by three Coys. B. C. & D was to be evacuated, while that held by A Coy. was to be handed over to the 62nd Bde. att. 9th Division.
This Coy. which consisted of about 120 men (including the supporting platoon of B Coy. 9th Welch) handed over the line to 19 men of the 1/7th West Yorks and it was due to this severe weakening of the garrison of such important ground that the CRATER was lost the next day (16thinst.)
During the night of the 15th/16th the Battn. withdrew without molestation, according to the orders outlined above - At dawn it was taking up positions astride the KEMMEL - WYTSCHAETE road, just E. of PARRAIN FARM where Bn. H.Q. were established. The Battn. was here in support to the 9th Welch who were holding the line from a point just S. of SPANBROEKMOLEN CRATER to SPY FARM.
B Coy. was ordered to dig a series of posts in the N.E. corner of N.28.b. and A. C. & D Coys. were distributed in partly dug positions over the area N. & S. of PARRAIN FARM.
The Battn. remained in these positions for two days - during which time SPANBROEKMOLEN was lost.
On the night of the 17th/18th the Battn. relieved the 9th Welch and elements of the 5th S.W.B. in the front line - which ran from the X roads N.29.w.2.5. south to N.29.d.2.8. - thence W. to N.28.d.5.6.
This line was taken over with three Coys. in the front line (A. B. D. from left to right) and 1 Coy. in support just South of STORE FM. (C Coy) - the line was nowhere continuous but touch was maintained everywhere
The day was quiet (18th April) until 1.30 p.m. when the enemy started to shell the support line fairly heavily, and the front line intermittently.

The French had, at about 6 p.m. the night before, attempted to advance & capture SPANBROEKMOLEN. This attempted was unsuccessful, although elements of the 22nd Division reached the western edge of the crater. A number of French troops remained in our front line throughout the following day (April 18th) and apparently it was owing to some movement in the French advanced trenches West of the CRATER that the enemy put down this heavy barrage at 1.30 p.m. It lasted till 5.30 p.m. when the French withdrew from their advanced line & the enemy followed - Our left Coy. put up the S.O.S. and the Artillery opened on their S.O.S. lines. At the same time the enemy who had been advancing with difficulty under our L.G. & rifle fire (which was slightly hampered by the French on their retirement) apparently decided to advanced no further. He was then about 300 yards away & opened heavy M.G. fire on our trenches, sweeping the parapets of the front & support lines. However soon afterwards the situation quietened down completely.

The whole operation on the afternoon of the 18th seemed in the nature of a demonstration more than anything else; the enemy were nowhere in large numbers, & I fancy that movement on the part of the French in their front trenches was largely responsible for the liveliness during the latter part of the day.

On the night of the 18th/19th the Bn. was relieved by the 22nd French Divn. & on relief moved to billets near ABEELE, via LA CLYTTE & RENINGHELST, where they arrived about 9.30 a.m.

H.W. HOUSE,

Major,
Commdg. 6th Wilts R.

April 25th 1918.

Appendix.

APPROXIMATE CASUALTIES to the 6th Wilts R. between the 10th April & 20th April 1918 -

1. No. going into the line on the night of the 7th/8th April:- 11 Officers. 580 Other ranks.

2. No. coming out of the line 12th April -
5 Officers. 175 Other ranks.

Reinforcements & attachments. 5 Officers. 270 Other ranks.

3. No. going into the line on the night of the 13th April - 10 Officers. 380 Other ranks.

4. No. coming out of the line on the night of the 18th/19th April - 4 Officers. 250 Other ranks.

H.W. HOUSE, Major,

April 25th 1918.   Commdg. 6th Wilts R.

HQ. 58th Inf Bde.　　　　　　　SR 1/6

Herewith Narrative of events
from 10th April — 20th April
during operations near LYTSCHAETE.

H.W. House
　　　　Major
　　　f/Lt Colo R.
　　　　　April 25. 1918.

1.

6th Shillelah Yeomanry Battn. The Shillelah Regt.

Narrative of events during the operations from April 10th — April 20th 1918.

On the night of the 9th/10th April the Battn. was holding a subsector of the line just east of the MESSINES-WYTSCHAETE ridge - with it's right on the WAMBEKE & it's left on JUNCTION BUILDINGS (exclusive). The position was held by two Coys (A & B) which were distributed in depth - each with two platoons in the front line of posts & 2 strong platoons in support. C & D Coys were in reserve about 2000 yds behind the front line. Bn. HQ were at TORREKEN FM. About 3.30 am. fairly heavy shelling on the whole subsector began, consisting of H.E. & gas shells. This continued practically without intermission the whole day though no gas shells fell after about 5.30 am. About 6 am. the shelling which was much heavier on the subsector of the Battalion on our right reached a climax, and the enemy under cover of a very thick "Scotch mist" attacked the 57th Bde. on the right & apparently forced it's centre Battn. back on to its reserve line. The left Bn. of the 57th Bde. (the 10th Warwick R.) evidently had it's right flank turned, & the success of the attack was so sudden that a portion of the Warwicks were forced to fall back in a northerly direction on to our right flank - the WAMBEKE formed the natural boundary between the 57th & 58th Bdes - & just North of it ran a long, thickly boarded-up, but shallow communication trench - MANCHESTER St. Between VERNE Rd. & GUN farm was a system of flooded shallow trenches, which C Coy occupied since...

2.

to form a defensive position, while half the support platoon of B. Coy was utilised, with any parties of the 10th WARWICK R. which came across the BEKE, to man MANCHESTER St as a long defensive flank.

The 4th Coy (D Coy) was used to stiffen up the defence of the right flank of this Bn which was so dangerously exposed.

The whole Bn orchestra was subjected to heavy shelling and a large part of it to M.G. & rifle fire throughout the day, the M.G. & rifle fire coming from the high ground South of LOMBEKE round ANZAC FARM.

The Bn maintained its positions everywhere until 4.30 pm that afternoon. At 3.30 pm the enemy was massing 2000 yds east of our post line — & a partial attack developed, but was unable to materialise owing to our vigorous Lewis & gun & rifle fire.

At 4.30 pm orders were received by the Battn on our left (1st RWF) to evacuate the post line of posts; & as this order emanated from Bde the post line held by this Bn was also abandoned, although the order for this to be done never reached the post line from our Bn HQ.

A strong position was then taken up by the two posts Coys on the line of the supporting points. The enemy advanced about 5.30 pm & was on

3.

original front line, but was unable to approach nearer than 600 or 800 yds owing to our active Lewis gun & rifle fire.

About 6 p.m. the enemy organised strong attacks on our right & left flanks. The orders to withdraw on to the Reserve line never reached the front line Coys, so our positions on the support line were held until the enemy had completely surrounded the two front line Coys, a few elements of which, only, managed to work through to our own lines.

The reserve Coy, which had been heavily engaged on the right flank, fell back fighting onto the high ground WEST of OOSTAVERNE. Batt^n HQ Coy which was utilised in an attempt to strengthen the right rear, was also engaged heavily in fighting in which the C.O., Major Monreal, was mortally wounded & the 2nd in Command Capt Gartewaite wounded.

During the night the survivors of the Batt^n rallied in positions of the front between the DAMMSTRASSE & WYTSCHAETE; 75 stragglers were collected & sent up to GRAND BOIS, where Capt Rentoul had established B^n HQ. The remainder of the day was spent in collecting & reorganising the Batt^n.

On the 12th April the Bn was withdrawn to ROSSIGNOL CAMP, near KEMMEL.

4.

270 Reinforcements were waiting here & the Battn. was reorganised mustering 450 strong — and moved to BARBADOS Camp LA CLYTTE for the night.

At 10.30 am the next day orders were received to stand by ready to move & a quarter of an hour later the Battn. was ordered to march to a position of readiness between LA CLYTTE & KEMMEL east of the main road. At 12 noon C.O's were warned that the Bde. would take over the line that night from the S. African Bde. Details of the relief could not be given till 4.30 pm at the S. African Bde. HQ & then were very complicated. The Bn. was to take over from 4 units — a portion of the 4th S. African Bn., the whole of the 1st S. African Bn., 2 Coys of the 10th R. Warwick R. & 1 Coy of the 5th S.W.B. The front it was to take over was about 800 yards & included the extremely important high ground at the SPANBROEK -MOLEN CRATER.

The Bn. marched up from its position of readiness and although virtually all Companies were in position by 3 am, the relief was not reported complete till 6 am.

The Bn. was disposed as follows from left to right. A. Coy. two platoons, front line one, support. East of SPANBROEKMOLEN CRATER.

B, C & D Coys each two platoons in the front line & one in support, from left to right.

On the right of D Coy were the 12th R.I.R and on

5.

the left of A Coy were the 3/th R.W.F.

Bn HQ were 300 yards in rear of the front line
just W. of SPANBROEKMOLEN CRATER.

The 14th April was an abnormally quiet day; the
enemy artillery was more or less inactive except
in the area round Bn HQ, which eventually later
moved to REGENT St DUG OUTS, N.29.c central.

On the night of the 14th it was decided that
the dispositions of the Bn required adjustment.
It was decided to push up the whole of A &
D Coys into the front line, & withdraw the whole
of B & C Coys into support, B on the left &
C on the right, covering A & D respectively.

In addition to ensure the security of the
SPANBROEKMOLEN the G.O.C. placed 1 Coy of
the Welch at the disposal of O.C. 6th Wilts R.
The O.C. this Coy (B. Coy) was accordingly ordered to
send 1 platoon to be in close support to A Coy
just East of the CRATER, and place the remainder
of his Company in a position West of the CRATER,
from which it would be ready to launch an
immediate counter-attack against the high
ground should this be lost, or reinforce the
front line.

These alterations in the dispositions of
the Battn were carried out during the night of
the 14th/15th.

At dawn on the 15th the enemy opened
a heavy H.E. barrage on the whole subsector

particularly along the support line, and in the area round REGENT St DUG OUTS.

About 5.45 am. the S.O.S went up on the left Coy front. The enemy were attacking on the right Coy front, and on the front of the Battn on our right. The attack failed to reach our front line, but the enemy succeeded in penetrating the front of the 12th R. IR. who were at the time attempting to carry out a withdrawal, using their left flank as a pivot. The enemy occupied RE & SHELL FARMS and made it necessary, first, for half of C Coy to move up & occupy a line, running approximately E & W, north of SHELL farm and securing the right Coy, in order to safeguard its right flank, to bend its right back on to the left of C. Coy's front line.

The line therefore was intact, though thinly held; the enemy snipers and machine guns were extremely active, &, being close, hindered movement, & the organisation of our new front on the southern flank.

On the remainder of the Battn front enemy movement was vigorously checked by snipers & lewis guns. In spite of very heavy shelling in the earlier part of the day, casualties on the left half of the front were slight.

As the line was rather held on the right, it was decided to dribble 1 platoon of B Coy of the 9th Welch up into the front line held by C. & D Coy, and to move 1 platoon up into support behind D Coy's left. This was successfully done.

That night orders were received to withdraw from the front line South of the SPANBROEKMOLEN CRATER. This meant that the line occupied by three Coys, B, C & D was to be evacuated, while that held by A.Coy was to be handed over to the 62nd Bgd. att. 9th Division. This Coy which consisted of about 120 men (including the supporting platoon of B.Coy 9th Welch) handed over the line to 19 men of the 1/7th West Yorks and it was due to this severe weakening of the garrison of such important ground that the CRATER was lost the next day. (16th inst).

During the night of the 15th/16th the Battn withdrew without molestation, according to the orders outlined above. By dawn it was taking up positions astride the KEMMEL-WYTSCHAETE road, just E of PARRAIN FARM where Bgd HQ were established. The Battn was then in support to the 9th Welch who were holding the line from a point just S of SPANBROEKMOLEN CRATER to SPY FARM.

B.Coy was ordered to dig a series of posts in the N.E. corner of N.28.b, and A, C, & D Coys were established in partly dug positions over the area N & S of PARRAIN FARM.

The Battn remained in these positions for two days — during which time SPANBROEKMOLEN was lost.

On the night of the 17th/18th the Battn relieved the
1st Welch and elements of the 5th S.W.B. in the
front line – which ran from the X roads N.29.b.
2.5. South to N.29.d.2.8. – thence West to
N.28.d.5.6. –

This line was taken over with three Coys
in the front line, (A, B, D from left to right)
and 1 Coy in support just South of STORE FM.
(C.Coy) – the line was nowhere continuous but touch
was maintained everywhere.

The day was quiet (18th April) until 1.30 pm
when the enemy started to shell the support line
fairly heavily, and the front line intermittently.

The French had, at a hour before the night
before, attempted to advance & capture
SPANBROEKMOLEN. This attempt was
unsuccessful, although elements of the
22nd Division reached the western edge of the
Crater – A number of French troops remained
in our front line throughout the following
day (April 18th), and apparently it was
owing to some movement in the French
advanced trenches west of the CRATER that
the enemy put down their heavy barrage
at 1.30 pm. It lasted till 5.30 pm. when
the French withdrew from their advanced
line & the enemy followed – Our left Coy put

up the S.O.S., and the Artillery opened on their S.O.S lines. At the same time the enemy, who had been advancing with difficulty under our L.G. rifle fire (which was slightly hampered by the French in their retirement) apparently decided to advance no further. He was then about 300 yards away & opened heavy M.G. fire on our trenches, sweeping the parapets of the front & support lines. However, soon afterwards the situation quietened down completely.

The whole operation on the afternoon of the 18th seemed in the nature of a demonstration more than anything else; the enemy were nowhere in large numbers, & I fancy that movement on the part of the French in their front trenches was largely responsible for the liveliness during the latter part of the day.

On the night of the 18th/19th the Bn was relieved by the 22nd French Div. & on relief moved to billets near ABEELE, via LA CLYTTE & RENINGHELST, where they arrived about 9.30 a.m.

H. H. Hohn Major
Commdg 5th Rifle Bde.

April 25th 1918.

Appendix

APPROXIMATE CASUALTIES to the 6th Wilts R
between the 10th April & 20th April 1918.

---

1. N⁰ going into the line on the night of the 7th/8th April
   11 Officers. 580 other ranks.

2. N⁰ coming out of the line 12th April.
   5 Officers. 175 other ranks.

Reinforcements. 5 officers 270 other ranks.
attachments.

3. N⁰ going into the line on the night of the 13th April.
   10 Officers. 380 other ranks.

4. N⁰ coming out of the line on the night of the 18th/19th April
   4 officers 250 other ranks.

H. Honeyman
Comm⁰ᵈᵍ 6th Wilts R.

April 20th 1918.

30TH DIVISION
21ST INFY BDE

6TH BN WILTS REGT
MAY 1918

Vol 35.

21/30

CONFIDENTIAL

War Diary

of

6" (Service) Battn. Wiltshire Regiment.

May 1918.

Volume. 35.

6th BATTALION. WILTSHIRE REGT.

May 1st to 10th. Brigade holding the Iron-Bridge - VOORMEZEELE sector. Battalion in support to 9th R.W.F. & 9th Welch.
DISPOSITIONS. 3 Coys. in G.H.Q. 2 line.
1 Coy. with Bn.H.Q. in Reserve W. of CAFE BELGE.
A quiet period, except for intermittent shelling of the G.H.Q. 2 line (southern portion in particular).

Night May 10th/11th. Brigade relieved by the 56 Inf.Bde. Battalion relieved by the 9th Cheshire Rgt.

May 11th. Battalion in camp near ST. JANS de BIEZEN.

May 12th. Bde. moved to HERZEELE AREA. Battalion in billets near HERZEELE.

May 13th. Battalion absorbed into the 2nd Battn. Training staff of 6th Bn. proceeded to 30th Division , BOYSCHERE en route for Le TREPORT under command of Major J.A. BUSFIELD.

Army Form C. 2118.

WAR DIARY
or
INTELLIGENCE SUMMARY.
(Erase heading not required.)

Instructions regarding War Diaries and Intelligence Summaries are contained in F. S. Regs., Part II. and the Staff Manual respectively. Title pages will be prepared in manuscript.

Place	Date	Hour	Summary of Events and Information	Remarks and references to Appendices
HERZEELE	13th		Battalion was formed into Training Centre Battalion and transferred to 30th Div. Army Authority 2nd Army G. 867 dated 9. 5. 15. Major J. A. Busfeild D'm Cheshire Regt. took over Command. The following Officers, Major J. A. BUSFEILD. LT. R. F. FORBES. 2nd LT. C.H.H. JENKYN. 2nd LT. C.W. WIGGINS. 2nd LT. J.W. CAYGILL. 2nd LT. W.S. ROYLE. 2nd LT. C. BARLOW and 45 Other Ranks left HERZEELE at 9 am and proceeded to LEDERZEELE NR St OMER. Battalion attached to 21st Inf. Brigade.	
HAZEBROUCK				R.X.7.
HAZEBROUCK				R.X.7.
LEDERZEELE	14th		Awaiting orders to entrain	
HAZEBROUCK SR	15th			R.X.7.
do	15th		Battalion entrained at RUDRICQ Station at 6.30 pm	R.X.7.
MELLEVILLE	16th		Battalion detrained at WOINCOURT 7.30 am and marched to Billets at MELLEVILLE.	R.X.7.
DIEPPE 1/1 am, am	17th		Training commenced with 3/189th Inf Regt American Army. Inspection in afternoon of Battalion by Divisional Commander	R.X.7.
do	18th		Training	R.X.7.
do	19th		Sunday Church Parade Battalion attached to 90 Inf Bde Bn Divn.	R.X.7.
do	20th		Training	R.X.7.
do	21st		Training	R.X.7.
do	22nd		Training	R.X.7.
do	23rd		Training	R.X.7.
do	24th		Training	R.X.7.

Army Form C. 2118.

WAR DIARY
or
INTELLIGENCE SUMMARY.
(Erase heading not required.)

Instructions regarding War Diaries and Intelligence Summaries are contained in F. S. Regs., Part II. and the Staff Manual respectively. Title pages will be prepared in manuscript.

Place	Date	Hour	Summary of Events and Information	Remarks and references to Appendices
MELLEVILLE	25th		Training.	
	26th		Sunday. MAJOR C. WALLACE joined for duty.	
	27th		Training. 2nd Lt. J.W. CAYGILL & 5 O.Ranks attached to 114th Amc.N. for training.	
	28th		Training.	
	29th		Training. CAPT. F. McLACHLAN, LT. L.C. MORGAN joined for duty.	
	30th		780 Paraded "Celebration Day" of American Army. CAPT. F. McLACHLAN attached to 114th Amc.N.	
	31st		Route March. Lecture by Lieut. Col. Campbell on Bayonet Fighting.	

Mch. DIEPPE. 1/10, 000.

JW Scofield
Lieut Colonel
Commanding 6 Wiltshire Regt.

www.ingramcontent.com/pod-product-compliance
Lightning Source LLC
Chambersburg PA
CBHW081352160426
43192CB00013B/2390